PARENTING
IN A
DIGITAL
WORLD
A STEP-BY-STEP GUIDE TO INTERNET SAFETY

Author Clayton Cranford, M.A.

Copyright Information

Use of Materials

Readers are encouraged to use the ideas from this book and other Cyber Safety Cop educational materials in their personal and professional lives. We ask that readers give proper acknowledgement to Cyber Safety Cop when they use any examples, ideas, stories, language, or practices that they learned from our program and let others know how to reach our organization—without giving the impression they are authorized or certified by our organization unless they truly are. For any questions about acknowledgement or use, please e-mail info@cybersafetycop.com or call (657) 206-6070.

Disclaimer

Products and company names mentioned from hereon out may be trademarks of their respective owners and organizations.

This book expresses the views and opinions of the author. The author will not be held responsible or liable for any damages caused or alleged to be caused either directly or indirectly by this book. The content within the book is provided without warranties. The views and opinions expressed in this book by the author are in no way representative of the author's current or previous employers.

Photography

Gina Marie Photography
http://www.gmariephoto.com

ISBN 978-1514162798

Dedicated to My Family

The Cyber Safety Cop program, my work fighting human trafficking, and this book would simply not be possible without the love, patience, generosity, and help from my family. This book is dedicated to them:

To my indomitable wife, Gretchen, who has given me constant and unwavering support, our two boys, Clay and Zachary, who love technology and are my "goofballs," now and forever.

To my parents, Otis and Patricia who taught me to do good in the world, serve others, and be true to myself. To my two older brothers, Michael and Matthew, who introduced me to computers and technology when the Commodore 64 was state of the art. And my sister Kimberly, who's memory is a sweet presence in my life everyday.

And finally, this book is also dedicated to the parents, teachers, principals, law enforcement officers, and counselors who are dedicating themselves everyday to keeping our children safe. Thank you.

Contents

Introduction

On a bright, sunny first day of school, I walked through the front doors of my Middle school and was immediately greeted by the office manager.

"Deputy Cranford, thank goodness you are here!"

Those words, and their urgency, were not what I wanted to hear walking through the door of my new job as a School Resource Officer. I found Jessica, a 7th grade student, sitting in the counseling office, doubled over in a chair weeping uncontrollably. The school guidance counselor, with a look of sadness and concern, sat next to her rubbing her back, trying to calm the distraught twelve-year-old girl.

Through the tears, Jessica told me that over the summer her boyfriend had asked her to send him a nude picture of herself; which is known among students as "sexting." She didn't want to do it, but he pestered her relentlessly until she did. After recounting her story, she framed her torso by placing one hand below her chin and the other at her waistline and said, "I sent him this."

Jessica and the boy, she sent the image to, were no longer "dating." She believed that he had sent the image to at least one other boy, his close friend. After hours of investigation and interviewing Jessica's ex-boyfriend and his friend, I was able to delete the image from his phone. He promised he did not send the image to anyone. His friend had seen the image, but it had not been sent to him by text or email.

What could I tell Jessica and her mother? I could not guarantee that the image was truly gone. The sad truth of the matter was once Jessica sent that nude image of herself to her boyfriend; it was completely out of her control. Her boyfriend could have sent that image to one friend, or fifty. Only time would tell.

What advice could I give to Jessica and her mother? "Don't do that again," wasn't going to cut it. There had to be more. There had to be a way for Jessica's mother to adequately supervise her daughter's online activities, and for Jessica to learn how to navigate cyber space safely.

That experience and hundreds thereafter, formed the Cyber Safety Cop program. I created the Cyber Safety Cop program to teach parents and students how to be safe online and with all forms of social media.

The goal of this book and the Cyber Safety Cop Workshops are one in the same: Parents will gain an understanding of how important social media and social networking is to their children. They will understand the unique threats that exist online, including: cyberbullying, impersonation, identity theft, sexting, sexual predators, human trafficking, digital reputation management, pornography, and other high-risk behaviors.

Most importantly, parents will be given tools and resources to help them properly supervise their

children online. They will walk away with a strategy that includes: guidelines to be implemented in their home that will immediately make their children more cyber safe.

Students will learn about privacy and why controlling who has access to their social networks is key to a safe and enjoyable experience online. They will, maybe for the first time, come to understand what their digital reputation is and why establishing a good, or bad one, can have lifelong consequences. Finally, they will learn how to deal with bullies and other negative behavior when it inevitably comes their way.

I promise you, what I promise every parent or student who attends one of my Cyber Safety Cop Workshops: You will put down this book empowered.

The threats are real and sometimes disquieting, as thousands of teens like Jessica can attest, but by the end of this book you will have a plan. And something else really special will happen too. You will have amazing conversations with your child about something that is intimately important to them—technology and social media. You will have a window into your child's world. You will see things in your child's social network that will give you amazing insight into what is important to them. Some of it may cause pause, and some of it will affirm what you already know. Either way, it will help you draw closer to your child.

The Cyber Safety Cop Plan

EDUCATE YOURSELF
- Go to a Cyber Safety Cop Parent Workshop. Page 80
- Subscribe to the Cyber Safety Cop Newsletter. Page 81
- Review games and apps before you download them for your child at www.commonsensemedia.org

TALK WITH YOUR CHILD
- Show interest in your child's online world and games.
- Talk about your safety concerns.
- Be open and direct.

USE PARENTAL CONTROLS
- Follow the directions in this guide to activate the safety settings in your operating systems, search engines, and games.
- Monitor your kids' use and their screen time.
- Install a monitoring/filtering application on your child's device.

SET RULES AND EXPECTATIONS
- Use Internet Usage Contract. Page 7
- Respect age limits on social media. Page 13
- Enforce consequences when appropriate.
- Periodically physically review the content on your child's device.
- Charge your child's devices in your room at night.

FRIEND AND FOLLOW
- Know all of your child's user names and passwords to all of their accounts.
- Friend or follow your child on social media.

CREATE BALANCE
- Establish "screen time" limits for school nights and for weekends. Page 15
- Plan family time without electronics.
- Curb your own bad digital habits.

Cyber Safety Cop's
Internet & Mobile Device Usage Contract

In a poll reported by the National Crime Prevention Council, more than 80 percent of teens surveyed said they either did not have parental rules about Internet use, or found ways around the rules. Cyber Safety Cop wants to turn that statistic around. The number one safety factor in any child's life is a parent who will talk to them and help them develop coping strategies. The Internet & Mobile Device Usage Contract is a tool to help parents start an on-going conversation with their children about social media and the Internet. The contract does the following:

- Sets boundaries around what behavior is and is not appropriate.

- Sets expectations about what their child should do when encountering inappropriate content or behavior.

- Clearly defines your child's expectation of privacy, which starts at zero and is left to the discretion of the parent.

- Sets reasonable consequences if the child does not abide by the rules of the contract.

- Creates a safe environment which will encourage a child to confide in their parent(s).

How Do I Use the Contract?

The Cyber Safety Cop Internet & Mobile Device Contract is not unlike other Internet contracts you can find online with a casual Google search. What is different about this contract is how you use it.

Sit down with your child and read each line of the contract with them. At the end of each line, follow up with an open ended question. It will go something like this:

> *"Number one, I will not give my name, address, telephone number, school name, or parents' names to anyone I meet on the computer. **Why do you think that is a good idea? Have you ever seen someone do that before? What could happen if you told a stranger what city you lived in?**"*

Do this with each point of the contract. When you get to the final point of the contract, tell your child what their consequences will be if they do not follow the rules of the contract. Be reasonable in your discipline. Make sure you can carry out the consequence you levy. Don't be the parent who does not have a plan and in distress says, "You are losing your phone forever!" Well, at some point that parent will have to cave in and give the phone back. Not a good precedent to set.

Finally, you want your child to come to you if they see or do something inappropriate online. Only 1 in 10 children will tell their parents about something inappropriate they saw online. If they think they will lose their phone or access to the Internet if they tell you, they may hide what happened and hope you never find out. To encourage your child to be upfront with you, you must include *grace* in this contract. Your conversation with your child might go something like this:

> *"I am giving you a mobile device and social media because I trust you. I also know you will make mistakes, or you will see something inappropriate that you know I would have a problem with. Here's the deal: If you come to me immediately and tell me what happened, I will help you. I will not punish you. If you forget to tell me or hide it from me, I will punish you."*

Use this Contract as a spring board to begin an ongoing discussion with your child about being safe online. Download a copy at www.cybersafetycop.com/resources

Cyber Safety Cop's
Internet & Mobile Device Usage Contract

I understand that using the Internet or my mobile device is a privilege, which is subject to the following rules:

1. I will not give my name, address, telephone number, school name, or parents' names to anyone I meet on the computer.

2. I must tell my Mom and/or Dad all of my social networks' usernames and passwords. They have access to all of my files/apps (anything on my device) at any time.

3. I will not download anything or install apps or games without first asking my parent(s).

4. I understand that some people online pretend to be someone else. I will never let someone into my social network that I do not already have a real face-to-face relationship with.

5. I will not fill out any form online that asks me for any information about myself or my family without first asking my parent(s).

6. I will not buy, order anything online, or give out any credit card information without first asking my parent(s).

7. I will never write or post anything online that I would not want my parents to see. I will not use profanity or offensive language.

8. I will promote _____ (a cause or charity) that helps others in my social network as a condition of having a social network.

9. If someone sends me any pictures or any e-mails using bad language, mean rude, or threatening words, I will not respond and tell my parent(s).

10. If someone asks me to do something that I am not supposed to do, I will not respond and tell my parents.

11. I will not call anyone I meet online or in person, unless my parent(s) say it is okay.

12. I will never meet in person anyone I meet online, unless my parent(s) say it is okay.

13. If I receive an inappropriate photo from someone, I will not respond or show my friends. I will immediately tell my parent(s).

14. If anyone I meet online sends me anything in the mail or by email, I will tell my parent(s). I will not keep online secrets from my parent(s).

15. If I make a mistake or see something inappropriate, I will tell my parent(s) as soon as possible.

16. I will respect the house rules for technology and screen time.

17. If I do not follow the above mentioned rules of this contract, I will accept the consequences my parent(s) give me, which may include (but is not limited to) losing access to the internet, my phone, or any other electronic devices.

_____   _____
Signature of child   Date   Signature of parent   Date
After signing, post visibly by computer

Social Media Defined

When you think of social media, I am willing to guess that Facebook or Instagram first come to mind. If we only look at Facebook and Instagram, two of the most popular social media platforms in the world, we will draw too narrow a definition and miss all the other places children communicate.

A broader, more inclusive definition of social media should be:

> **Social Media** is any device or application that allows a user to communicate with another person.

This new definition of social media will hopefully open your eyes to a much bigger world. These devices and applications are really just portals to other people. The portal may be an web cam chat room with strangers or something innocuous as Words with Friends. For parents to properly monitor their children's social networks, they must first realize that social media does not only exist on smart phones, tablets, and computers, but exists in a whole new world of social networking that is now just being created.

The Problem With Social Media

Social media and socially embedded technology is a moving target. Today's hot social media app could be easily replaced tomorrow with a new competitor.

After investigating cyberbullying and other social media related crimes over the years, I have traced the root of all the threats on social networks to two basic problems inherent in nearly all social media platforms.

> Children can communicate and meet people outside their parent's sphere of influence and control.
>
> Children and adults can communicate anonymously without any accountability, removing the natural inhibition or fear of getting caught.

Today's teen is sitting in their room with a mobile device in her hands. They have the Internet and social media access literally at their finger tips. Our social media connected teen is sharing intimate details about herself to potentially 2.5 billion people on the Internet. An unsupervised, unfiltered Internet will leave a child open and vulnerable to threats and attacks that the parent and child are completely unprepared for.

Now that you understand what the two basic problems with social media are, you will look at the Internet in a new and completely different way. You will quickly see how a social network's privacy setting, or lack thereof, can allow strangers into your child's life. New social media applications are being created daily. Developers are looking for the next big thing. They are pushing the boundaries. They are trying to entice teens by creating new and exciting online experiences. Often these new exciting environments are not safe.

Action Plan

- Take an inventory of all the electronic items in your home or child's life and how they connect to the Internet(e.g., Wifi, hardline, cellular, or a combination)?

- Do your child's devices have parental controls?

- Can your child communicate with another person with this device? How do they communicate (e.g.,Text, camera, or voice)?

- Are the people they communicate with a defined group of people that you know, (i.e. private server for Minecraft for just friends), or strangers?

- Can you filter or block the device's ability to communicate with others? For example, some games allow you to turn the chat feature off, or you can unplug the microphone to disable the voice-over-IP chat?

Managing Your Online Reputation & Privacy

Teens share everything. How they feel about life, a new song, their science homework, pictures of themselves, where they'll be hanging out with friends, or possibly doing something inappropriate. Parents need to be aware of what their children are sharing in their social networks, how it affects their digital reputation, and the long-term consequences.

When a parent gives their child access to social media, they should help them create a positive digital reputation. The added benefit of doing this is finding a positive outlet for your child's creativity, community service, or entrepreneurial interests.

Keys to Shaping a Positive Digital Reputation

Be selective of what you publish online.

You should only publish information you are completely comfortable with others seeing. I tell students, before you hit the send button ask yourself: "If I put this post or image on the side of a bus and drove it around the city with my name on it, would I be embarrassed?" If the answer is yes, then do not send it. Look for opportunities to publish information that will lead to a reputation that will make you and your parents proud. Stay away from using words, symbols, or images of violence, guns, weapons of any kind, alcohol, drugs, pornographic or suggestive material, inappropriate language, and derogatory or racist comments.

It is permanent.

Once you publish something on the Internet, it does not belong to you anymore. It can be copied, reposted elsewhere, and used for some unintended purpose. It is true, you can delete posts on social media sites, but often before this can be done, others have screen-shot your post, and are saving it on their device to be posted later.

Privacy is an illusion.

A private post or message is never truly private. Social media apps that claim to delete your content after the recipient reads it (e.g., Snapchat) are easily circumvented. I have personally investigated many incidents where the sender believed their communication was private and later learned their message was shared with others.

Manage your digital reputation.

Periodically perform online searches of your name and nickname and see what comes up. Don't just use one search engine, but a variety of them. If you find unflattering photos of yourself, delete them, or ask the person who posted it to remove it. Your friends might be tagging you in images and posts that you have nothing to do with. Monitor how other people are using your name.

Privacy

Every social media app or platform should have a "Privacy Setting." A privacy setting allows the user to decide who gets to read the text, images, or video they publish in their network. Many social networks like Facebook or Instagram have two privacy choices: Private or Public. A privacy setting is like the front door to your home. If your social network is set to "Private," then your door is closed and locked. Someone who wants to come into your home has to knock on your front door. You look out through the peephole and decide whether you want to let them in. If it looks like someone you know, or someone you can trust, you open the door to them. If it is someone you don't know, the door remains shut. If your privacy setting is set to Public or Open, then your front door is left wide open with an invitation for anyone to enter.

Your child should not have a follower that they, or you, do not know (i.e., A real life, face-to-face relationship). Clear communication with your child is fundamental to helping them make the right decisions online. Use the following points of discussion to educate your child while making your expectations about their online privacy clear.

Action Plan

- Make sure each one of your child's social media accounts has a privacy setting and set to "private."

- Explain why it is dangerous to have people you don't know in your social network.

- Ask your child, "What's the upside to keeping a total stranger in your network?" Follow up with, "Do more likes make you a more popular person? Does it make you feel better about yourself? Should it?"

- Review each follower with your child.

- If your child does not have a real life face-to-face relationship with a "friend" or follower, then they must be removed or blocked. All new requests should only be granted to people your child has met in real life and can vouch for.

When Should I Give My Child Social Media?

Possibly the most common question I get from parents is: "Should I let my [fill in the age]-year-old have [fill in the social media site]? This is also one of the most common problems that I run into when investigating cyberbullying or an online threat—the child or bully was given social media too early. Early on in my cyber-threat investigations, I was shocked to find the majority of my cases involved elementary students. In fact, these 10 to 12-year-olds were engaging in this activity more often than their middle and high school counterparts combined. Often, the perpetrator and victim alike were allowed to have a social media accounts, or created the account themselves without their parents knowing.

Every social media site has a minimum age requirement in their user agreement. I have indicated the minimum age for each application on page 24, along with Popular Apps, and whether they are safe for children. Facebook and Instagram's User Agreements state you must be at least thirteen-years-old to have an account. Even Facebook and Instagram think your ten-year-old child is too young. I would challenge parents to ask themselves: Is thirteen old enough for my child?

There are two good reasons why a parent should never give their child social media before the User Agreement allows, and perhaps even wait a bit longer.

Setting Standards and Not Sending the Wrong Message

Any child who has Facebook or Instagram knows the minimum age to have an account is thirteen. If a parent allows their child to have social media before the minimum age, they aren't fooling anyone. What kind of message are we sending to our children if we click "Agree" to the User Agreement when it states: "You will not use [this social media site] if you are under 13?" We are telling our children rules don't matter, even the small ones. We are missing out on an important parenting moment.

The Teen Brain is Not Built for Making Good Decisions

This will not come as a surprise to parents, but young people make poor choices. Science has finally explained why. Dr. Jay Giedd at the National Institute of Mental Health in Bethesda, Maryland looked at the brains of 145 normal healthy children by scanning them at two-year intervals. Giedd found that in an area of the brain called the prefrontal cortex, the brain appeared to be growing before and through puberty and doesn't mature until into a person's mid-twenties. The prefrontal cortex sits just behind the forehead and is responsible for rational thought and decision-making. As the prefrontal cortex matures, teenagers can reason better, develop more control over impulses and make better judgments. (Giedd, 1999) Research has also discovered that decision making during the teen years, and while the prefrontal cortex is still developing, shifts to the limbic system of the brain. The limbic system of the brain is involved in instinctive "gut" reactions, including "fight or flight" responses. These studies suggest that while adults can use rational decision-making processes to navigate through emotional decisions, adolescent brains do not yet have the hardware to think through things in the same way. (Brownlee, 1999) For example, a classmate at school makes fun of Jimmy's shoes on Instagram for hundreds of fellow students to see and comment on. An adult looks at this situation and easily dismisses it as childhood nonsense. However, Jimmy's immature prefrontal cortex may not be able to coolly deal with this situation. His emotional feelings of embarrassment may win out, resulting in Jimmy lashing out on Instagram. The conclusion and implication should be clear: We are giving children who lack the ability to make good decisions the opportunity to destroy their reputation on a permanent medium — the Internet.

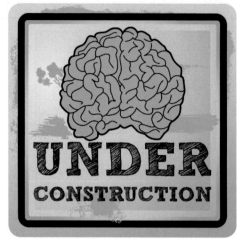

Next time your teenager says, "I'm old enough to make my own decisions," you have the scientific authority and backing to say, "No you are not!" Case closed.

Create Balance In Your Child's Technological Life

Convenience and constant access provided by mobile devices, especially smartphones, has resulted in 92% of teens going online daily. 24% say they go online "almost constantly," according to a new study from Pew Research Center. More than half (56%) of teens (ages 13 to 17), go online several times a day, and only 12% report once-a-day use.

Kids, ages 8 to 18, are spending an average 44.5 hours per week in front of screens. Parents are increasingly concerned that screen time is robbing their children of real world experiences. Nearly 23% of youth report that they feel "addicted to video games" (31% of males, 13% of females). These are the results of a study of 1,178 U.S. children and teens (ages 8 to 18) conducted by Harris Interactive (2007) that documents teen video game use at pathological levels.

The following are some suggestions for helping create balance in your child's world:

- **Use social media as a tool for promoting a charity or social cause.** Teach your child that having a voice is a powerful thing. Use it to reach and inspire others for good. Have them promote a fundraiser or a community service meet-up on their social network.

- **Create limits.** Limit the amount of time your child can be on screens (any device that has a screen) on a school night, and perhaps even the weekend. For example, 2-hours on a school night and 4-hours on the weekend. Doing chores or going outside to exercise may earn more screen time.

- **Likes should not equal self-esteem.** When a teen posts an image in their social network they get instant feedback in the form of "Likes" or positive comments. Research has shown us that once the teenage brain has linked a behavior to a reward, it continues to seek the reward again and again. Talk to your child about why they are posting images. Is it to share something they are proud of, or to garner validation from others?

- **Be the person you want your child to be.** Take technology breaks and engage with your child. Board games and other structured time with the family are priceless opportunities.

- **Don't be afraid to be the bad guy.** Make a plan and stick to it. Boundaries are essential for your child's safety and wellbeing. Don't be surprised when you feel push back from your child when you implement these new rules. These guidelines will help your child's social skills and personal growth.

The American Academy of Pediatrics recommends that children should be limited to less than 2 hours of entertainment-based screen time per day.

Download Cyber Safety Cop's Screen Time Worksheet to help establish screen time limits in your homes. http://cybersafetycop.com/Resources

Online Predators use Social Media to Exploit Children

In December of 2014, the parents of a ten-year-old girl alerted Cleveland Police Department that sexual predators were contacting their daughter through her iPad.

The iPad was intended for schoolwork, but once social media applications like Snapchat and Skype were installed, the tablet became a portal to a dangerous world. After about a month of unmonitored use, her mother checked the device and was horrified to learn that 16 men had been attempting to manipulate her daughter into sexual situations.

The ten-year-old schoolgirl was first contacted by a man on Snapchat, who after talking about things a ten-year-old would be interested in, turned the conversation to sex. Predators who try to sexually exploit children for the purpose of producing child pornography often share that pornography, or access to the child, with other predators. The number of predators who were contacting their daughter grew in a short span of time. The predator's methodology was a textbook use of social media to manipulate and exploit this young girl.

The anonymity and the global nature of the Internet make its use by sexual predators a predictable threat, although most parents are unaware of the danger it poses to their children. The pedophiles in this case are likely based in the UK and other countries overseas, making identifying and prosecuting them difficult. Police Detectives from Cleveland Police are working with Snapchat and Skype in the hope of tracking them down.

The young victim told many of the men that she was ten years old, but this only encouraged them to ask for explicit images. One of the predators begged her to disrobe and send him nude images and video. He begged, "Open cam baby … plzzzzzz I like sex. What problem r u no interest to sex." Another of the unidentified men offered to transfer money to the ten-year-old so that she might travel to meet him. (Dailymail, December 27, 2014)

Everyday, children in your community are being targeted, snared, and manipulated by a world of sexual exploitation. They are enticed, and sometimes physically coerced, into selling themselves for sex. It is called human trafficking. It is modern-day slavery, without the chains and shackles of a century ago, but it is real and happening right under our noses. A community that says, "We don't have that problem," is a community that has not looked for it. How are these traffickers and pimps gaining access to your children? You don't see them cruising the streets of your neighborhoods. They do not need to. They are being invited into your child's life, into your homes, and into your child's most private and intimate

conversations, through the Internet and social media.

In my Cyber Safety Cop Parent Workshop, I ask parents where they believe the safest place for their child is. I always hear the same answer: Their home. What is the fear of allowing their child unsupervised outside the home? The general concern among parents is the possibility of their child meeting someone the parent doesn't know – someone dangerous. Although this possibility does exist, the rate of violent crime across the country has dropped significantly in the last twenty years. The chance that a teen will ever come into physical contact with a sexual predator in their neighborhood, let alone be snatched off the street, is very low. When we look again at the picture of a child sitting alone in the safety of his or her room, we see something new. The child sitting on their bed now has a mobile device in their hands, with Internet and social media access. Our social media-connected teen is not only exposed to the people in their neighborhood, or even the population of the United States, but to roughly 2.5 billion people on the Internet. This translates into millions of sexual predators who have access to children in their own home.

Social media platforms are places where predators can actively stalk children, but there are other websites that are passively waiting for children to stumble onto them. Pornographic website chat rooms, or classifieds websites are all places where predators are waiting for the curious child to explore. Backpage is a popular online classified ads website, second only to Craigslist. A young girl, looking to get "discovered" as a model or musical talent, may respond to one of many ads on Backpage that claim to be a legitimate talent search. These ads are neither legitimate nor safe, and have been the source of minors being sexually assaulted and trafficked into the commercial sex industry. The young girls who go to these parties or talent searches are unwittingly walking into a well constructed trap. The "agent" or "event promoter" is setting up a situation where these girls are being coerced into having sex with men at these events. The coercion is aided with alcohol and drugs, lowering inhibitions enough to manipulate their victims into complying with their orders.

The trafficker may not be who you expect. They come in many forms. Many pimps and traffickers will employ other students, your child's peers, as recruiters. A young girl will be more likely to go to one of these parties if they were invited and accompanied by another female student.

The parents of the ten-year-old Cleveland girl believed that they took all sensible precautions to protect her. They turned on some of the iPad's parental settings to filter content. Unfortunately, they did not go far enough. In this chapter, I will outline how online predators are using social media to exploit children, and offer some truly sensible safety measures to keep your children safe.

To begin, we must understand who the enemy is and their capabilities. The online predator/pedophile is networked with millions of other like-minded individuals who share their techniques and experiences with each other. They know how to identify the most vulnerable victims and what techniques to use to

groom children into sending nude images or videos. In some cases, an accomplished pedophile can manipulate the child, build a relationship, and have the child voluntarily meet or run away with them.

To keep your child safe from these predators, we need to have a basic understanding of how they operate:

- **Online predators look for children who are emotionally vulnerable or who do not appear to have a stable home life.** The most vulnerable are children who are dealing with a broken home, runaways, or who are in the Child Welfare System. Parents must be aware that every child is potentially vulnerable, no matter their family composition or socio-economic level. Children share their thoughts, feelings, likes, and dislikes freely on social media. It does not take the predator long to discover who is having problems at home or with key relationships in their lives.

- **The predator listens and sympathizes with the child.** These predators are skillful manipulators, and the children they prey on do not have the maturity or life experience to counter their advances. They tell the child what the child wants to hear, not what they need to hear. When a teen laments about being grounded for a week by their parent, the predator tells them their parent was wrong or stupid, and they should have the freedom to do what they want. The predator begins building an "us-against-them" relationship that drives a wedge between the child and their parents.

- **The predator intensifies the relationship by seducing the child.** The seduction phase of the manipulation is key to the pedophile's success. The predator further grooms the child through attention, flattery, affection, kindness, and even gifts. He will make the child feel special. Initial target selection for this phase is very important. Emotionally vulnerable children are craving love and acceptance. The pedophile knows that a properly manipulated and groomed child will not care that he is older. He does not have to coerce the child into sending him nude images or meet him. What makes this so dangerous is that the victim, the child, helps conceal the relationship from their parents.

- **The predator introduces sex into the conversation.** Depending on the progression of the third phase, the introduction of sex into the conversation may occur gradually or rapidly.

Online Predators use Social Media to Exploit Children Continued

How Do I Identify Human Trafficking?

Human trafficking can often go unnoticed, even by individuals interacting with a victim on a regular basis. Recognizing the "redflags," or indicators, can help alert parents, school administrators, and staff to a human trafficking situation. The Department of Homeland Security (DHS) has identified warning signs of a teen who is being trafficked. Recognizing the signs is the first step in identifying potential victims. No single indicator is necessarily proof of human trafficking.

Behavior or Physical State:

- Does the child have unexplained absences from school, or has the child demonstrated an inability to attend school on a regular basis?

- Has the child suddenly changed his or her usual attire, behavior, or relationships?

- Does the child suddenly have more (and/or more expensive) material possessions?

- Does the child chronically run away from home?

- Does the child act fearful, anxious, depressed, submissive, tense, or nervous and paranoid?

- Does the child defer to another person to speak for him or her, especially during interactions with authority figures (this may include an adult described by the child as a relative, but may also be a friend or boyfriend/girlfriend)?

- Does the child show signs of physical and/or sexual abuse, physical restraint, confinement, or other serious pain or suffering?

- Has the child been deprived of food, water, sleep, medical care, or other life necessities?

- Is the child in possession of his or her own identification documents (e.g. student identification card, driver's license, or passport), or does someone else have them?

Social Behavior:

- Does the child have a "boyfriend" or "girlfriend" who is noticeably older?

- Is the child engaging in uncharacteristically promiscuous behavior, or making references to sexual situations or terminology that are beyond age-specific norms?

- Can the child freely contact friends, family, or his or her legal guardian?

What Should I Do if I Suspect Someone is Being Trafficked?

If you suspect that a person may be a victim of human trafficking, please call the Homeland Security Investigations Tip Line at 1-866-347-2423 (24 hours a day, 7 days a week, in over 300 languages and dialects) or submit a tip online at www.ice.gov/tips.

You may also call the National Human Trafficking Resource Center at 1-888-373-7888 to get help or connect with a service provider in your area. The Center is not a law enforcement or immigration authority and is operated by a non-governmental organization.

Non-law enforcement personnel should never attempt to directly confront a suspected trafficker or rescue a suspected victim. Doing so could put both your and the victim's safety at risk. By immediately informing law enforcement of your suspicions, you can safely assist in the recovery of the victim and the dismantling of the trafficking operation.

School administrators and staff who suspect a trafficking incident should follow their school district's established protocol for such matters. Schools that do not have such procedures in place should consider adopting a formal protocol on how to identify the indicators and report suspected cases to law enforcement. Your protocol should be developed in collaboration with school district leadership; federal and/or local law enforcement; mental health, child welfare, or victim services providers; and other appropriate community partners. (DHS.gov, 2015)

DHS offers free online Human Trafficking Awareness Training at:

http://www.dhs.gov/xlibrary/training/dhs_awareness_training_fy12/launchPage.htm

Cyberbullying

What is Cyberbullying

The phenomenon of bullying is nothing new. Any parent who was bullied as a child can recount that experience with great detail. Cyberbullying does share certain characteristics with traditional schoolyard bullying, but there are important and distinct differences. As we will see, these distinct differences make cyberbullying in many ways more psychologically hurtful and physically taxing than traditional bullying.

My parent workshop does not include a definition of bullying. The term bullying is chronically overused. It is being used to describe virtually any situation between children that involve mean-spiritedness or hurt feelings. I do not want my parents to be distracted with a label. I want them to focus on the behavior. Rude, aggressive, hurtful behavior needs to be addressed whether it occurs once or repeatedly. Why have a definition at all? Because, behavior that qualifies as bullying is different and significant. It is more serious, in both its effect on the victim and even the bully.

Anyone working in the school system, kindergarten through high school, knows hurtful words and mean-spirited play make up a majority of student-to-student interaction. Is every one of these incidents a bullying incident? If every anti-social behavior is bullying, then everyone is a victim. In this context, bullying has lost all meaning. Can a one-time hurtful message impact a student to the point of causing significant psychological distress? The answer is, yes. Is it bullying? A good definition might help clear up this question.

Every major child health or anti-bullying organization has published their own definition of bullying. I believe one of the best and meaningful definitions of bullying is provided by Stopbullying.gov, a federal government website managed by the U.S. Department of Health & Human Services.

> Bullying is unwanted, aggressive behavior among school-aged children that involves a real or perceived power imbalance. The behavior is repeated, or has the potential to be repeated, over time.

Cyberbullying does not neatly fit into the above definition of bullying. It does not require the bully to be bigger or stronger than the victim. The Internet is the great equalizer of power. Everyone has an equal voice; therefore, the imbalance of power is transitory at best. A single comment or image can become viral, growing exponentially. Although it is a single act, it can have the same effect as a repeated attack on the victim.

Affects of Cyberbullying

Victims of cyberbullying tell me they feel helpless. Blocking the bully or turning off their phones does not solve their problem. It is like a malevolent force, growing in power, turning their friends against them. The ever-present nature of the Internet and cyberbullying creates a low constant level of stress in the

victim. The body responds to stress by dumping cortisol into the blood stream, creating a feeling of fight-or-flight. The victim's nervous system is constantly under duress, even sleep is difficult to achieve when wondering what someone is saying about you online. Children caught in this syndrome of cyberbullying-induced stress can have all the symptoms of Post Traumatic Stress Disorder (PTSD).

It's not just the victim that needs help. After investigating hundreds of cyberbullying incidents, I have learned that the bully needs as much help, maybe even more help, than the victim. A 2012 study, published in the Journal of Abnormal Child Psychology, found there was a clear link between bullying and PTSD. The study of 963 teens aged 14 and 15 in Norwegian schools found symptoms of the disorder in about 33 percent of the students who said they were victims of bullying. The study also found that those with the worst symptoms were a small group of students who, in addition to being victims of bullying, frequently bullied fellow students themselves. The goal of the juvenile justice system is not to lock up kids or throw them away. The goal is to intervene, educate, and restore.

How to Respond to a Cyberbullying Incident

I encourage parents to empower their children with the tools necessary to resolve a bullying incident on their own. Of course, this may not be possible in every case, especially when violence is involved. My experience is most students want the opportunity to resolve their conflicts with other students. Unfortunately, many parents never give them the opportunity to do it. They immediately call the teacher or principal to intervene. The following are steps I give students to deal with rude or bullying behavior in my Student Workshop:

- **Tell the bully that "It's not funny, it's harassment, and if it doesn't stop I will take it to the next level."** When you ask a bully why they were bullying another student, they will invariably tell you, "It was just a joke." I tell students in my Student Workshop to take that argument away from them. Telling the bully that you will "take it to the next level," is preferable to saying, "I'm going to tell on you."

- **Do not retaliate.** If a student gets a rude or threatening message, they should not respond. It's that simple. I have seen the victim face school discipline alongside the bully because they responded in kind.

- **Tell a trusted adult**. What is a trusted adult? I tell students, a trusted adult is an adult that will stop what they are doing and help you. Ask your child to make a list of trusted adults in their life. You may be surprised by who they include on the list, and who they leave off.

- **Document the abusive behavior.** If possible, take a screen shot all of the mean, rude, or threatening messages immediately. If the bully thinks you are going to report them to the school or police, they may try to cover their tracks by going back and deleting their remarks or their entire account.

- **Report abuse to the hosting site.** See how to report abuse on a comprehensive list of sites and services on page 75. If your child receives a message that is a threat of violence, call your local police agency immediately.

- **Block the bully from contacting you.**

Phone Security & Privacy
10 Tips for Parents and Students

1. **Add a password to your phone.** It might be inconvenient to type a number into your phone each time you want to use it, but losing your phone without that protection could lead to a far greater headache.

2. **Use a "find your phone tool."** Certain software and apps, including Find My iPhone (and Find My Phone for Android), make it easy to find your phone if you lose it, and help anyone who finds it to return your phone to you.

3. **Reject email and social media requests from strangers.** Criminals might send friend requests to people they don't know to gather information about them. While most people will ignore or reject the request, a small portion will accept, and those are the people who criminals target.

4. **Check privacy settings on apps.** Some apps request a lot of information from you, including your location and passwords or access to other apps or your text messages. If they don't need all of that information (and why would they?), then deny access.

5. **Avoid fraudulent Wi-Fi networks.** A fraudster sets up a Wi-Fi network in a public place. The WiFi name looks legitimate (i.e., "coffee_shop_wifi"), but instead of simply providing free Wi-Fi, he's using the signal to collect information (e.g., usernames and passwords) from the people around him who log onto the network.

6. **Use strong passwords.** People often reuse the same passwords for multiple sites, which can leave them vulnerable to hacking if one site gets broken into. Some passwords, like ones based on your birthday or mother's maiden name, are easy to figure out.

7. **Smart phones, just like computers, can get viruses and malware.** Don't download content or applications from unknown or unreliable sources on your mobile internet browser and consider installing a reputable anti-virus/malware app.

8. **Apps, 'Jailbreaking', and 'Rooting' can expose your device to threats.** Do you know where your third-party apps are coming from and do you trust the software author? Only accept Apps from authorized App stores.

9. **Keep your operating system and apps updated.** Download patches and update your computer and mobile devices. They do not only add new features, but also offer improved security.

10. **Disable locations services.** Apps like the Camera app use your GPS location and imprint your location on every picture you take. A stranger could take an image you have shared to some social media sites and learn where you live.

Popular Apps

Snapchat (13+) This extremely popular app which allows the user to send a picture, text, or video to another Snapchat user. What makes this app special is that the sender can assign a lifespan to the message, up to 10 seconds. **Problem:** This app gives the sender the impression that they can send a "snap" without a care or concern to the possible consequences of sending an inappropriate image or video. Snapchat is the number one sexting app. Images can be captured in a screen shot or by taking a picture with a second device. Additionally, teens might be using this app to hide conversations from their parents. Not safe for children.

Kik Messenger (+17) This instant messaging app is wildly popular among teens because it is a free cross platform app (it can be installed on just about any device, e.g., iPhone, iPod Touch, iPad, Android, or Windows phone). Your child doesn't need a cell phone service to use it. They only need WiFi. When teens send messages to their friends, they call it "kik'ing" a friend. **Problem:** A Kik user can create an account name that is not associated with a phone number, making authenticating a user's identity difficult. It also contains adult apps and content. Similar app: *TextNow or WhatsApp*. Not safe for children.

Tinder (+17) This app's primary purpose is to facilitate hooking-up and dating. 450 million profiles are rated every day. Tinder utilizes GPS location tracking to find people (strangers) near you. 13-17 year-olds now represent over 7 percent of the users on Tinder. **Problem:** Tinder makes it easy for your child to meet a complete stranger, possibly an adult, within walking distance. It also links to Instagram and Facebook. Similar apps: *Blender and Grinder.* Not safe for children.

Whisper (+17) This app allows the user to overlay an image with text to express their feelings anonymously. It does however display the area you are posting from and also allows the user to search for others posting near you. **Problem:** The anonymous nature of this app makes it ripe for cyberbullying. A user can post a picture of a fellow student and overlay derogatory text anonymously, a common tactic used by cyberbullies. The use of GPS to communicate with strangers nearby is very troubling. Similar app: *Secret*. Not safe for children.

Popular Apps continued

 Ask.fm (+13) This App allows users to anonymously ask or answer other user's questions. **Problem:** There are many documented cases of cyberbullying on Ask.fm that have lead to suicide. Not safe for children.

 Yik Yak (+18) Yik Kak is an app that allows users to post text-only (at least presently) messages, know as "Yaks," of up to 200 characters. The messages are viewed by the closest 500 Yakkers to the person who wrote the Yak. Yik Yak users are grouped together by their device's GPS location services. **Problem:** Yik Yak users are essentially anonymous. Yik Yak has been used to bully and threaten students. Not safe for children.

 Omegle (13+) Omegle is a free online chat website that allows users to communicate with strangers without the need to register. The service randomly pairs users in one-on-one chat sessions where they chat anonymously using the handles "You" and "Stranger." **Problem:** Omegle has a video chat that is not monitored for sexual content. The anonymous nature of this app has been known to attract pedophiles that want to expose themselves to children or interact with a minor that they have already groomed. Not safe for children.

 Fake Calculator (No age) Fake Calculator is a "vault" app. Vault apps appear to work as advertised (a game or utility app), but in actuality they are used to hide pictures, files, and other apps inside of them; hence the name "vault" app. Similar apps: *Vault-Hide, NQ Vault, App Lock, Vaulty, Hide it Pro, and Personal.* Not safe for children.

 Twitter (13+) This app is a social broadcast network that enables people and organizations to publicly share brief messages (140 characters per post) instantly around the world. Each post is referred to as a "tweet." **Problem:** Users can be bullied through replies, a embarrassing tweet can be shared and quickly go viral, no filtering of adult content, and children on Twitter can be contacted by adults.

 Facebook (13+) Facebook is the most popular social network in the world. Users share posts/video/photos. Facebook offers apps, games, text and video chat. **Problem:** Without supervision and proper privacy settings, children are potential victims of bullying, and sexual victimization by adults.

 YouTube (13+) YouTube is the worlds largest video sharing site. Users can upload their own videos. **Problem:** People can comment on other's videos, resulting in cases of cyberbullying. Privacy settings are confusing and without proper content filtering, children can be exposed to inappropriate content.

 Skype (13+) This app is one of the most popular video chatting and multiple communications platforms in the world. It is primarily used as a video chat platform. **Problem:** Without close adult supervision, children could have video chats with strangers they met on other sites.

 Tumblr (17+) This app is a cross between a blog and Twitter. **Problem:** A user's first Tumblr account is public, open to anyone to read. Adult content can not be filtered. Not safe for children.

 Instagram (13+) Instagram is the most popular image sharing social network for teens. **Problem:** Children can have adult followers. Cyberbullying through impersonation is relatively easy to do.

 Multi-Player Online Games (varies; check rating) New multi-player games are being released daily for desktop computers and mobile devices. They allow the player to interact with other players in a virtual world. **Problem:** In app purchases can be very expensive. It is also very addictive. Children are playing with strangers, possibly adults. Similar games: *Clash of Clans, World of Warcraft, & Wizard 101*

 Minecraft (No age limit) Minecraft is a wildly popular world building game that allows online play with strangers or private group play. **Problem:** In-game chat can have swearing and bullying behavior.

 Vine (17+) Vine is a social media app that lets you post and watch looping six-second video clips. **Problem:** Vine videos are public and adult inappropriate content can be found easily. Not safe for children.

 Periscope (18+) Periscope is a live video streaming app that links to the user's Twitter account. **Problem:** Adult content is easily found on Periscope. Children who use Periscope can be seen by strangers and adults that can live text chat with them while on camera. Similar app: *Meerkat*. Not safe for children.

 WhatsApp (16+) WhatsApp is an instant messaging app, similar to Kik Messenger. **Problem:** Users can be virtually anonymous. Cyberbullying and threats are difficult to trace back to the sender. Not safe for children.

Popular Apps continued

 Facebook Messenger (13+) This instant messaging app is linked to the user's Facebook account. **Problem:** Unsupervised messages can be used for bullying and sharing inappropriate images.

 Pinterest (13+) Pinterest is a social network to create digital bulletin boards and 'pin' images with links to the interesting things you find on the web to share with "friends" and "followers." **Problem:** Pinterest can link to Facebook and Twitter, causing privacy concerns.

 YouNow (12+) YouNow is a live broadcasting platform. Users can make a live video or watch channels produced by others. **Problem:** YouNow does have rules against nudity and sexual content, but a live feed can't be prescreened or rated, so there's no real way to know what your teen will view next. Not safe for children.

App & Game Ratings

The Entertainment Software Rating Board (ESRB) ratings provide guidance about video games and apps. http://www.esrb.org/ratings/

I also recommend using parent focused review websites like Common Sense Media. https://www.commonsensemedia.org

 EVERYONE
Content is generally suitable for all ages. May contain minimal cartoon, fantasy or mild violence and/or infrequent use of mild language.

 EVERYONE 10+
Content is generally suitable for ages 10 and up. May contain more cartoon, fantasy or mild violence, mild language and/or minimal suggestive themes.

 TEEN
Content is generally suitable for ages 13 and up. May contain violence, suggestive themes, crude humor, minimal blood, simulated gambling and/or infrequent use of strong language.

 MATURE
Content is generally suitable for ages 17 and up. May contain intense violence, blood and gore, sexual content and/or strong language.

 ADULTS ONLY
Content suitable only for adults ages 18 and up. May include prolonged scenes of intense violence, graphic sexual content and/or gambling with real currency.

 RATING PENDING
Not yet assigned a final ESRB rating. Appears only in advertising, marketing and promotional materials. It should be replaced by a game's rating once it has been assigned.

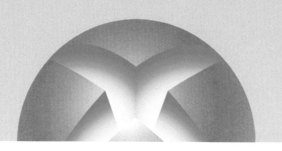

Parental Controls for Xbox 360

The Xbox 360 console lets you customize and manage your family's access to games, movies, and television content. The Xbox 360 parental controls can be used to control both the console itself and access to content on Xbox Live.

1. On your console, go to **Settings**, and then select **Family**.

2. Select **Content Controls**.

3. Change settings to **On**. If you have set a passcode on this console before, you will enter it now. If you have not set a passcode, you will be prompted to set one now.

   The console will provide you with preselected content settings. You can make changes to these settings on the menu items below.

4. I highly recommend setting up the **Family Timer** to help enforce screen time.

   Select whether you want to set a **Daily** or **Weekly timer**.

   Move down to the time period and use the left stick to increase or decrease the time period, then select **Continue**.

   Select **Save and Exit**.

   When the Family Timer is on, notifications will appear 1 hour, 30 minutes, 15 minutes, and 5 minutes before the time runs out. These give players sufficient warning so that they can save their games. However, when one of these notifications appears, you can add time or disable the timer altogether by entering your passcode.

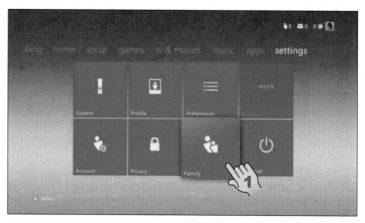
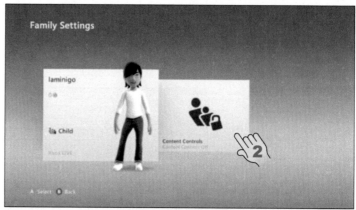
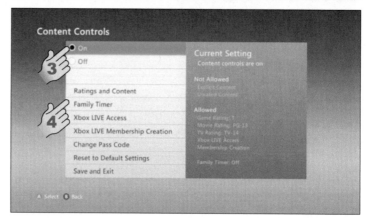

Set Online Safety & Privacy

5. Click your child's account.

6. Click on the right panel, **Privacy & Online Settings**. Select **Change Settings**.

7. Select a preset option for your child's appropriate age, **Teen**, **Child**, or **Customize**.

   Child will be the most strict security and privacy setting, blocking and filtering everything except online gameplay under the Activities menu. This is a good start.

   Teen setting allows online gameplay and web browsing.

8. If you choose **Customize**, you can make discrete changes to the privacy and online settings.

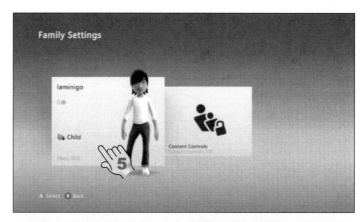

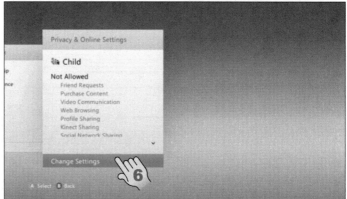

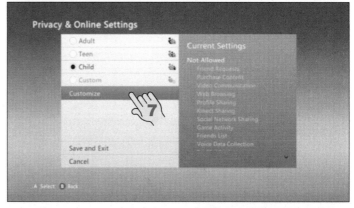

Parental Controls for Xbox One

When managing a child's account, privacy and online safety together make up what are called "Parental controls." These settings should be applied to the Microsoft account of each individual child, allowing parents to customize the Xbox One experience for each of their children. To start managing a child's privacy and safety settings, follow these steps:

1. Sign in to your console. On your controller, press the **Menu** button. Select **Settings**. Scroll right to Family, then select the child profile that you want to modify.

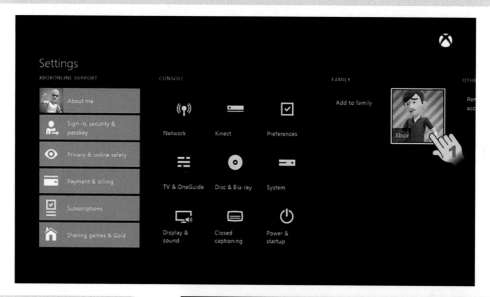

2. After you select your child's profile, you're shown the current privacy settings and content restrictions for that child. Select any default privacy setting to see its definition. You can keep the default setting as is, or you can customize it.

3. To customize a setting, select **Use, but customize**.

   You're presented with various customization options for each setting. Choose the options that best meet your family's online safety and privacy needs.

Parental Controls for Xbox One
continued

To view and customize the content restriction settings for your child, Press **B** on your controller to return to the previous screen.

4. Select a setting to find out more about it.

5. Select **Access to content** and apps to open a menu that will show you the details of your child's current content restrictions.

   Select the level of restriction that's appropriate for your child. (Teen or Child)

   By default, the level of restriction you set for your child is applied to searches, the store, and apps.

6. (Optional) To remove this restriction, clear the check box next to Hide listing in search, stores, & apps.

   The restriction will be removed for search, stores, and apps, but it will still be applied to actual content. When you're finished, press **B** on your controller to return to the previous screen.

View and customize the web filtering settings for your child

Web filtering lets you choose the kinds of websites your child can visit using Internet Explorer. To set a web filtering level for your child:

1. On your controller, press the **Menu** button.
2. Select **Settings**.
3. Select your child's profile.
4. Under Content Restrictions, select **Web filtering**.
5. Here, you'll see a menu that enables you to select the level of filtering that's appropriate for your child.
6. When you're finished, press **B** on your controller to return to the previous screen.

Parental Controls for PS4

To get the most of out the PS4's parental controls, you will want to make sure the adult has a Master Account, and the minor has a Sub Account. The Master Account controls what is and isn't accessible to Sub Accounts, and different rules can be created for individual Sub Accounts.

Creating A Sub Account for your child

1-2. Go to **Settings** icon ➤ **Parental Controls** ➤ **Sub Account Management**

You will now be asked to verify your PSN account by entering in your Sign-In ID (Email Address) and Password. Next, select **Create New Sub Account**, and press the Ⓧ button icon. Read the explanation of Sub Accounts. Then, select **next** and press the Ⓧ icon button. Select your child's Local User icon profile or click [Register User] to create a new local user profile. Then press the Ⓧ icon button. On the next screen, enter the Language and Date of Birth, and press the Ⓧ icon button.

Chat: The default setting is "Block" meaning chat is restricted. Sub Account holders will not be able to participate in text or voice / video chat with other PlayStation Network users.

Content Restriction: The default value is set to "On" meaning content will be restricted based on user age. If this restriction is removed, Sub Accounts will be able to buy and play any content, including content that is rated higher than their age, or is inappropriate for their age according to the ESRB rating system.

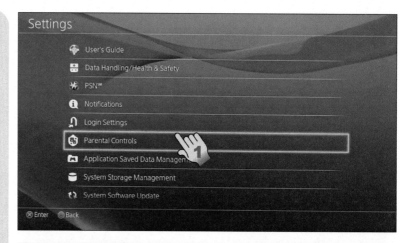

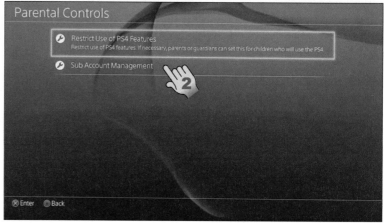

3. Return to the **Parental Controls menu**, and select **Restrict Use of PS4 Features**.

   In order to use these features, you'll need a 4-digit passcode. By default, the code is "0000," but you can alter it by choosing **Change Passcode**.

4. You can restrict games based on different levels on a scale of 1 to 11.

   Level 1 is for games that have not yet been rated.

   Level 2 allows only EC-rated (Early Childhood) games.

   Level 3 allows E (Everyone),

   Level 4 allows E10+ (Everyone age 10 and up),

   Level 5 to 8 allows Teen

   Level 9 allows Mature. The system is set to 9 by default.

5. You can also set the age limits for Blu-Ray and DVD movies under Blu-Ray Disc and DVD respectively.

6. Turn off Internet Browsing under Internet Browser

7. Block others from creating new users on your console under Select [New User] and log in to PS4.

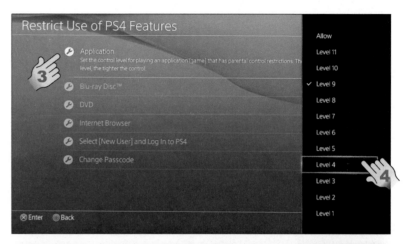

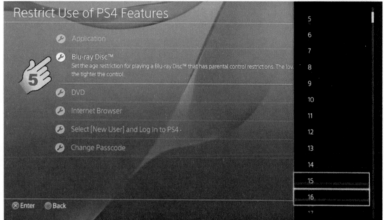

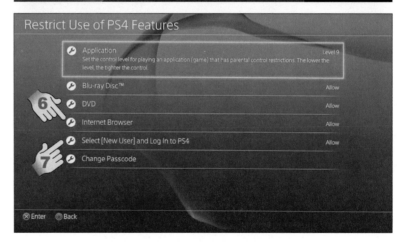

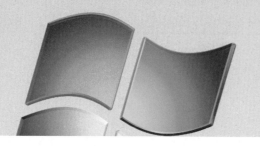

Parental Controls for Windows 7

1. Open **Control Panel** and click on **Set up parental controls for any user.**

2. Create or click on the child's account you want to set up

   Make sure to password protect your Administrator account, otherwise your child can turn off Parental Controls and use the computer without restrictions.

3. Under Parental Controls mark the radio button next to **On, enforce current settings**.

4. Then you can go through and control their computer time, games, and programs.

Adjust your computer's settings   View by: Category ▾

System and Security
Review your computer's status
Back up your computer
Find and fix problems

Network and

User Accounts and Family Safety
Add or remove user accounts
Set up parental controls for any user

Choose a user and set up Parental Controls

What can I do with Parental Controls?

Users

Child
Standard user - Parental Controls On
No Password

clayton
Computer administrator
Password protected

Set up how Child will use the computer

Parental Controls:
○ On, enforce current settings
○

Windows Settings

 Time limits
Control when Child uses the computer

 Games
Control games by rating, content, or title

Allow and block specific programs
Allow and block any programs on your computer

Current Settings:

Child
Standard user
No Password

Time Limits: Off

Game Ratings: Off

Program Limits: Off

5. Click on **Games** to set the ratings your child will be allowed to play.

6. Click on **Time limits** to control when your child has access to the computer.

7. Click **Allow and block specific program** to choose only the programs you want your child to use.

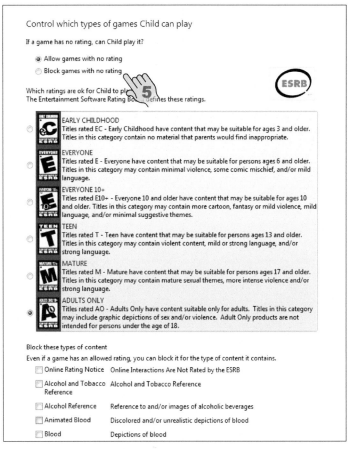

Control which types of games Child can play

If a game has no rating, can Child play it?

- ● Allow games with no rating
- ○ Block games with no rating

Which ratings are ok for Child to play?
The Entertainment Software Rating Board defines these ratings.

ESRB

EARLY CHILDHOOD
Titles rated EC - Early Childhood have content that may be suitable for ages 3 and older. Titles in this category contain no material that parents would find inappropriate.

EVERYONE
Titles rated E - Everyone have content that may be suitable for persons ages 6 and older. Titles in this category may contain minimal violence, some comic mischief, and/or mild language.

EVERYONE 10+
Titles rated E10+ - Everyone 10 and older have content that may be suitable for ages 10 and older. Titles in this category may contain more cartoon, fantasy or mild violence, mild language, and/or minimal suggestive themes.

TEEN
Titles rated T - Teen have content that may be suitable for persons ages 13 and older. Titles in this category may contain violent content, mild or strong language, and/or strong language.

MATURE
Titles rated M - Mature have content that may be suitable for persons ages 17 and older. Titles in this category may contain mature sexual themes, more intense violence and/or strong language.

ADULTS ONLY
Titles rated AO - Adults Only have content suitable only for adults. Titles in this category may include graphic depictions of sex and/or violence. Adult Only products are not intended for persons under the age of 18.

Block these types of content

Even if a game has an allowed rating, you can block it for the type of content it contains.

☐ Online Rating Notice   Online Interactions Are Not Rated by the ESRB

☐ Alcohol and Tobacco   Alcohol and Tobacco Reference
   Reference

☐ Alcohol Reference   Reference to and/or images of alcoholic beverages

☐ Animated Blood   Discolored and/or unrealistic depictions of blood

☐ Blood   Depictions of blood

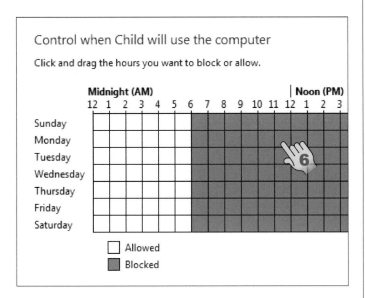

Control when Child will use the computer

Click and drag the hours you want to block or allow.

| | Midnight (AM) | | | | | | | | | | | Noon (PM) | | | |
	12	1	2	3	4	5	6	7	8	9	10	11	12	1	2	3
Sunday																
Monday																
Tuesday																
Wednesday																
Thursday																
Friday																
Saturday																

☐ Allowed
■ Blocked

Which programs can Child use?

- ○ Child can use all programs
- ● Child can only use the programs I allow

Check the programs that can be used:

File	Description
C:\Program Files (x86)\Common Files\microsoft shared\ink	
☐ mip.exe	Math Input Panel Accessory
☐ pipanel.exe	Microsoft Tablet PC Component
☐ TabTip32.exe	Tablet PC Input Panel Helper
C:\Program Files (x86)\Common Files\microsoft shared\MSInfo	
☐ msinfo32.exe	System Information
C:\Program Files (x86)\Common Files\Parallels\{88F796DA-4B1D-423	
☐ prl_net_inst.exe	Parallels Installation Utility
C:\Program Files (x86)\Common Files\Parallels\{B56B0EE1-8D82-4E3	
☐ prl_net_inst.exe	Parallels Installation Utility
C:\Program Files (x86)\Google\Chrome\Application	
☐ chrome.exe	Google Chrome
C:\Program Files (x86)\Google\Chrome\Application\35.0.1916.114	

Add a program to this list: [Browse...]

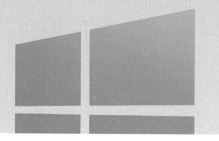

Parental Controls for Windows 8.1

Family safety is the security feature within Windows 8.1 that provides control over your children while the using PC. Family safety provides web filtering, time limits, application and game restrictions and control over website accessing.You can apply family safety in Windows to existing child account or to a new account.

1. Sign in to your PC with the administration account.

2. Click **Start** menu, click on drop down menu and select **PC settings**.

3. Select **Accounts**.

4. Other **Account**.

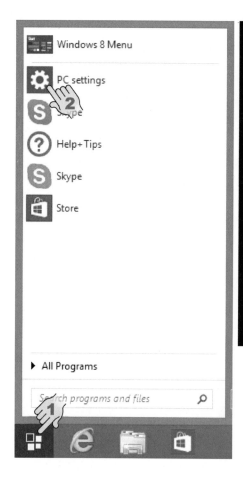

5. Do not fill in an email in the field. Click or tap on **Add a Child's Account**.

6. Here you can enter an email address for you child or not. The following steps are for adding an account without an email address.

7. Enter your child's name and create a password for them. I suggest always setting up passwords even if this is only used at home. Make sure to add the password hint but do not make the password hint the same as the password. Click the **Next** link at the bottom.

8. Your child's account is created. Now all you have to do is click **Finished**.

9. Now that you have your child's account all set up, it is time to set the Parental Controls. Windows 8.1 calls it, "Family Safety." You will now want to go back to the User Account Screen. You can get there by clicking the **Start** button 🔲 ➤ **Control Panel ➤ Set up Family Safety for any User**. The steps are the same as Windows 7 (Page 34).

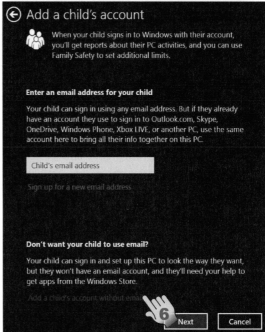

Parental Controls for Chromebook

First, log In With Your Own Parent Account. You can only use and manage Supervised Users account if they're linked to a main parent account — that's your account.

1. Click the menu button

2. Look for the **Signed in as** option to verify that your account is logged in.

3. Uncheck **guest browsing** and **restrict sign-in to the following users**. This will prevent your child from using the guest account or logging in with another Google account to bypass the Supervised Browsing restrictions.

4. Open Chrome's Settings screen from the menu and click the **Add User** button under Users. On a Chromebook, click the **Add user** option at the bottom-left corner of the login screen.

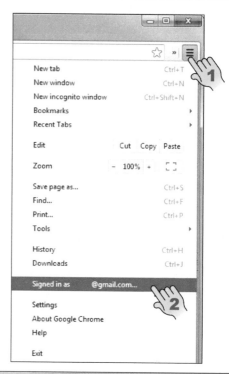

Parental Controls for Chromebook
Continued

5. Create a new user account and select **This is a supervised user managed by (your user account)**

6. You will be prompted to create a separate password for your child. Their entire user account will be locked down. Just sign out of the Chromebook and have them sign in from the login screen.

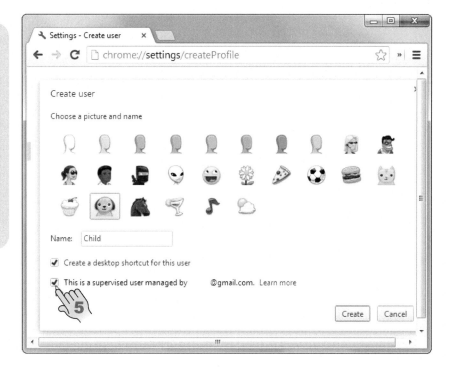

7. To manage the account restrictions, you'll need to visit Google's management tool at www.chrome.com/manage. Sign in with the username and password you associated with your own parent account, not the one associated with the child account. After signing in, you can modify the permissions for all your Supervised Users. You can also view their browsing activity and allow or deny any requests they've made to unblock websites.

8. When a user accesses a blocked site, they'll see a "you need permission" screen. They'll be able to click the Request permission button and any permission requests will appear on the management page. You can access this page from anywhere, so you could approve access to websites even if you're not at home.

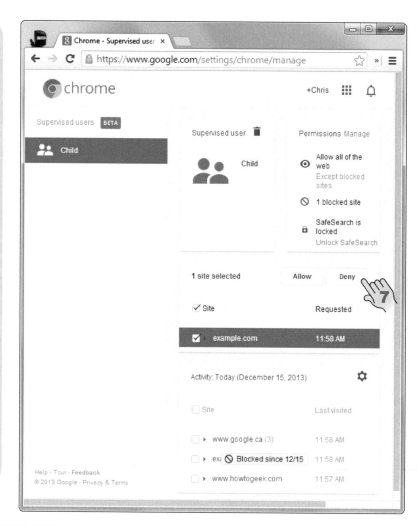

Parental Controls for Mac OS

1. Click on the **Apple symbol** 🍎 in the top left corner of your desktop screen.

2. Select **System Preferences** in the drop down menu.

3. Click on **Parent Controls** in the System Preferences window.

4. Create a new user account or modify the current account that is logged in.

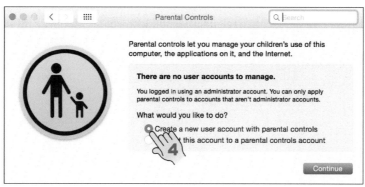

Parental Controls for Mac OS
Continued

5. Control Options

- **Apps** - Restrict what applications are available to your child.

- **Web** - Restrict web content or create a list of website which they can only visit.

- **People** - Control the joining of multiplayer games through Game Center and whether they can add their own "friends" on Game Center. Limit mail and messages to a select group of contacts.

- **Time Limits** - Set time limits.

- **Other** - Disable the built-in web camera and disable the changing of the account's password.

6. **Lock** to prevent further changes.

Parental Controls for iOS
(iPhone, iPad, & iPod)

1. Tap the **Settings** app.

2. Choose **General** for menu.

3. Scroll down to Restrictions. If you have never set up parent controls yet, it will show "off." Choose **Restrictions**.

4. Enable **Restrictions**.

5. Choose a passcode that only you know as the parent. Never share this with your child.

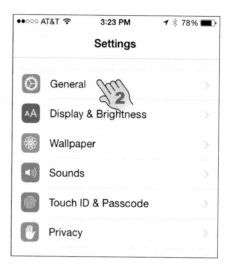

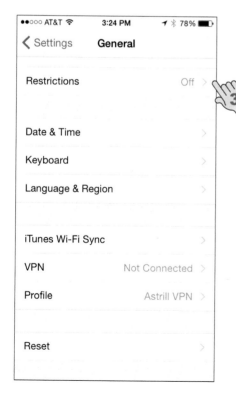

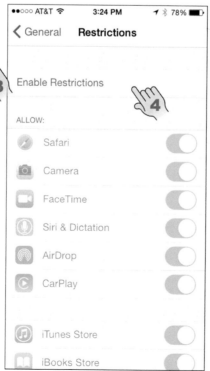

Parental Controls for iOS (iPhone, iPad)
Continued

6. The first section of the Restrictions menu will allow you to turn off select applications, such as Safari browser or the Camera (Green means on, greyed out means off). In the second section, be sure to turn off App Installing, deleting, and In-App Purchases.

7. The third section filters content from various sources. Tap on any of these to the follow-on screen.

8. Check the ratings you want to allow. The blocked ratings will be listed in red.

9. Scroll to the bottom of the menu to turn off Game Center's Multiplayer games and adding friends for children under 13 years old.

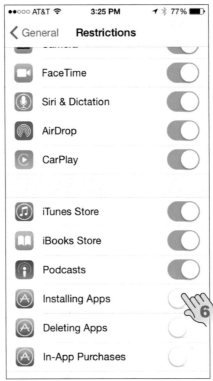

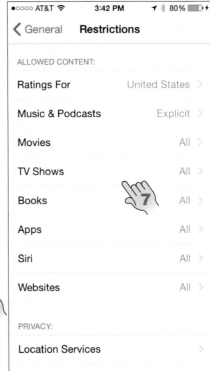

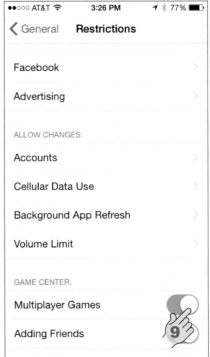

Parental Controls for Android OS
(Phones and Tablets)

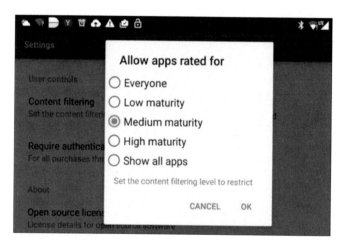

If your Android smartphone is running on Jelly bean or KitKat, then these controls will not be available. Check if there is any updates available to Lollipop: go to: Settings ➤ About Phone ➤ System Updates.

Step 1: Pull down the top right area of the home screen of your phone and tap on **Settings**. Scroll down and select **Users**. Then select **add user or profile**. There will be two options to create profile; a normal User profile and a Restricted profile, choose **Restricted profile**.

Step 2: If you have not done so already, a prompt will ask you to set up a screen lock for your Android phone. Tap on **Set lock**, then choose what type of passcode to use: a pattern, password, or PIN lock, and follow the given instructions.

Step 3: You will see a Settings icon which is located next to the **New profile**. Tap on it and give it a name.

Step 4: A list of apps installed on your Android phone will be listed with on/off toggles. By default, the restricted profile is unable to access these apps. Toggle on only the apps you want your child to have access to. You will see the web browsers installed on your phone included in the list. Toggle the browser off if you do not want your child to access the Internet.

Step 5: From the lock screen you will see your account is protected with a password, pattern, or PIN. Only those apps you switched on will be available to your child's account. If they tap the Google Play Store icon they will see a notification that says "you do not have the right permissions to use the Google Play Store".

Restrict in-app purchases in Google Play Store

Step 1: Launch the Google Play Store app on your Android device.

Step 2: Open settings menu and then go to **User controls**.

Step 3: A checkbox is next to the password. It needs to be checked. Doing so will require a password whenever someone attempts to download a paid app or purchase in-app extras.

Step 4: In the same menu you will see an option for **Content filtering**. There is an option to allow all apps or only those rated as high maturity, medium, low, or for everyone. Check the appropriate boxes and then click **Ok**.

Restricting app purchases in Google Play Store will not stop downloads from other third-party stores. To restrict other app download, go to Settings ➤ Security and disable the option of downloading apps from other sources.

YouTube Safe Search Desktop

To filter out adult and inappropriate content on YouTube, "safe search" settings must be put on every browser and YouTube app, on computers and mobile devices. Launch a browser window and type www.youtube.com in the web address bar.

1. Click the blue **Sign In** button in the top right corner of the screen and follow the prompts to sign in.

2. Once YouTube loads, Scroll down to the bottom of the page and click the **Safety** button.

3. Click **On**

4. Click the **Save** button. To lock these changes so no one can change them without your password, click "Lock safety mode on this browser." You'll be prompted to enter your password. Once that information is entered, the feature is locked and can only be unlocked by entering your password again.

You'll know the parental controls are activated when you do a search. Stated at the top of the search results will be the phrase "Some results have been removed because Safety mode is enabled." You need to do this for any and all browsers on your computer that you think your child might use to access YouTube. The process is the same.

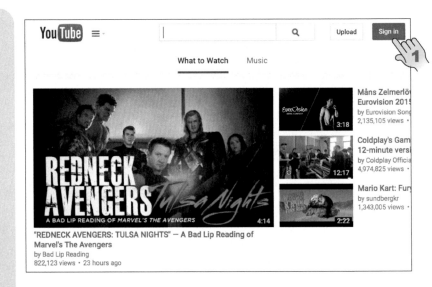

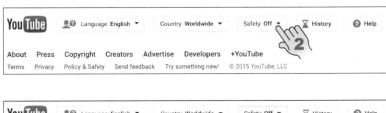

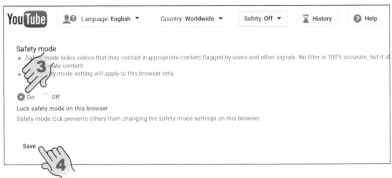

YouTube Safe Search iOS App

1. Open YouTube Mobile App. Slide your finger from left edge of the screen to the right to reveal the menu bar. Tap the Settings ⚙ cog.

2. Tap **Safe Mode Filtering**.

3. Select **Strict**.

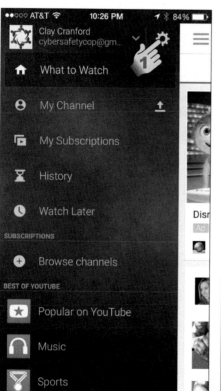
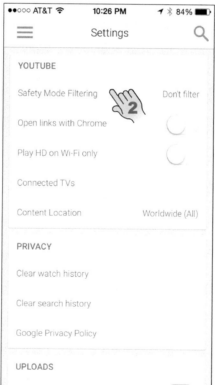

Google Safe Search
Apple Mobile App

1. Open the Google Mobile App. Tap the account profile picture.

2. Select **Safe Search**.

3. Select **Strict**.

Android Mobile App (not shown)

1. Touch ⋮ Menu ➤ Settings ➤ General

2. Under Safety mode check the checkbox to enable **Safety Mode**.

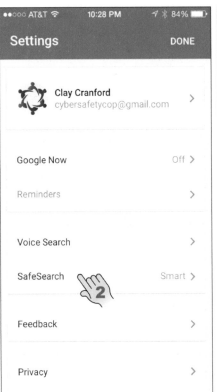
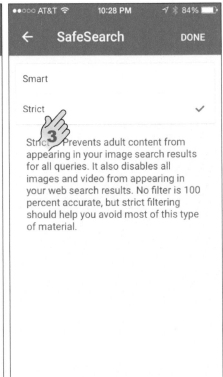

Google

Google Safe Search
Desktop Browsers

Google Safe Search settings filter out adult content showing up in search results. These settings must be applied to every browser on every computer.

1. Enable all third-party cookies in your browser's settings/preference panel.

2. Open the browser and navigate to google.com and sign in to your Google account. Then navigate to http://www.google.com/preferences. Check **Filter explicit results**.

3. Select **Lock SafeSearch** and sign back into Google.

4. You will see colored balls and "SafeSearch is locked" in the top right corner of the browser which will indicate that Safe Search is on. Reverse the steps to unlock.

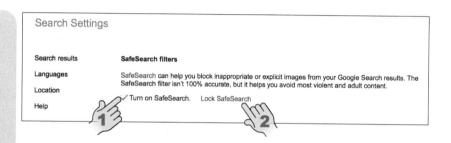

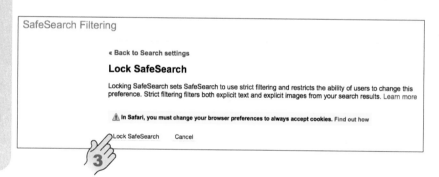

Bing Safe Search
Desktop Browsers

Bing is Microsoft's default search engine in Internet Explorer. Enable Safe Search to filter out adult content from search results.

1. Navigate to http://www.bing.com. Click the settings ⚙ icon in the top right corner.

2. Select **Strict**.

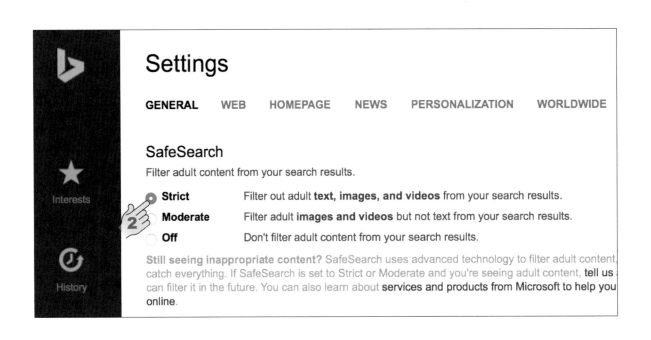

Settings

GENERAL   WEB   HOMEPAGE   NEWS   PERSONALIZATION   WORLDWIDE

SafeSearch
Filter adult content from your search results.

- ● **Strict**   Filter out adult **text, images, and videos** from your search results.
- ○ **Moderate**   Filter adult **images and videos** but not text from your search results.
- ○ **Off**   Don't filter adult content from your search results.

Still seeing inappropriate content? SafeSearch uses advanced technology to filter adult content, catch everything. If SafeSearch is set to Strict or Moderate and you're seeing adult content, **tell us** can filter it in the future. You can also learn about **services and products from Microsoft to help you** online.

Yahoo Safe Search
Desktop Browsers

1. Open the browser and navigate to Yahoo.com and sign in to your Yahoo account. Then navigate to https://search.yahoo.com/preferences. Click the settings ⚙ icon in the top right corner.

2. Select **Preferences**.

3. Select **Strict**.

4. Select **Lock**.

YAHOO!

Preferences
Languages
Search History

Search Preferences

SafeSearch
Yahoo SafeSearch helps you avoid explicit content in Yahoo Search results. We can't catch everything, but the filter helps keep adult content out. Learn more...

Strict - no adult content ▽

SafeSearch unlocked · Lock

Apple iMessage Privacy

Desktop Settings

1. Open the **iMessage** App.

2. Click on **Messages** in the app's tool bar to drop down menu.

3. Select **Preferences**.

4. Select **General**.

5. Uncheck **Notify me about messages from unknown contacts**.

Messages	File	Edit	Vi
About Messages			
Preferences...		⌘,	
Add Account...			
Log In		⌘L	
My Status		▶	
Change My Picture...			
Services		▶	
Hide Messages		⌘H	
Hide Others		⌥⌘H	

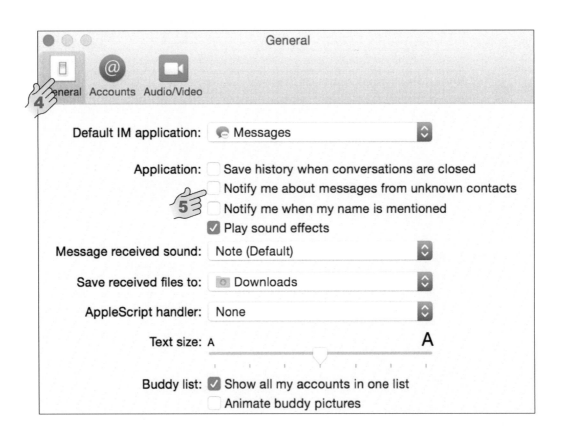

General

General   Accounts   Audio/Video

Default IM application: Messages

Application: ☐ Save history when conversations are closed
☐ Notify me about messages from unknown contacts
☐ Notify me when my name is mentioned
☑ Play sound effects

Message received sound: Note (Default)

Save received files to: Downloads

AppleScript handler: None

Text size: A ⎯⎯⎯⎯⎯ A

Buddy list: ☑ Show all my accounts in one list
☐ Animate buddy pictures

Apple iMessage Privacy

iOS Settings

1. Open the **Settings** App.

2. Scroll down and select **Messages** from the menu.

3. Turn on (green) **Filter Unknown Senders**.

To Block a Contact

4. Open the **Settings** App. Scroll down and select **Messages** from the menu. Select **Blocked**.

5. **Add** contact from your contact list to be blocked from calling or messaging your child.

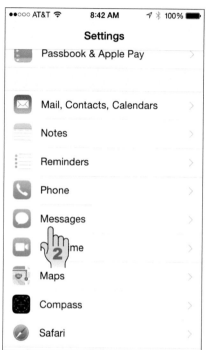

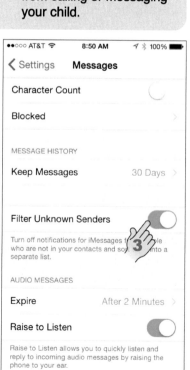

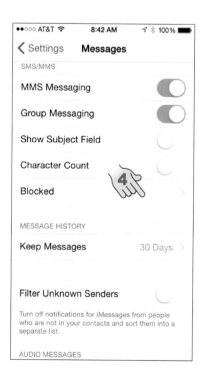

Apple iMessage Monitoring

If your child wants to use text messaging, iMessage is by far the safest choice. Do not let them use instant message apps like Kik or TextNow. You have two choices. One, you can keep you child under your iCloud account or you can create a unique iCloud account for them. I recommend keeping your child on your iCloud account so their phone number appears in your Messages menu. By following the directions below, you will be cc'd on all your child's messages.

1. Open the **Settings** App.

2. Scroll down and select **Messages** from the menu.

3. Select **Send & Receive.**

4. Click on your child's phone number. A check mark will appear next to it.

5. Go back to Settings by selecting **Messages.**

6. Then **Settings.**

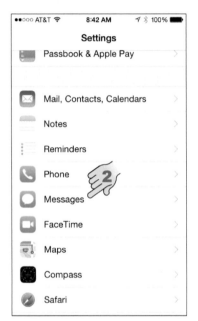

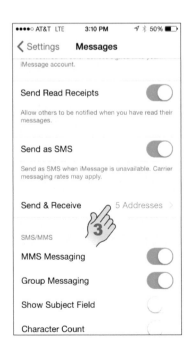

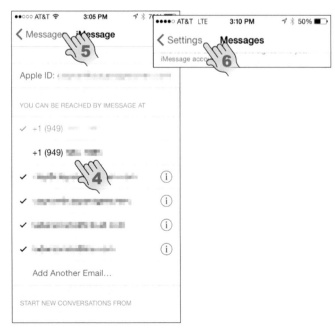

7. Select **General**.

8. Select **Restrictions** and enter your parental passcode.

9. Select **Accounts**.

10. Select **Don't Allow Changes**.

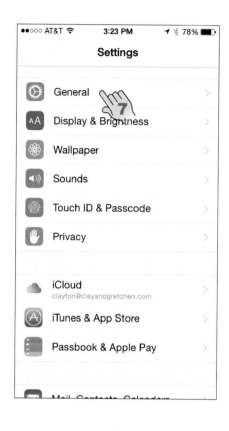

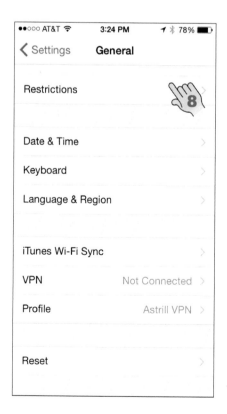

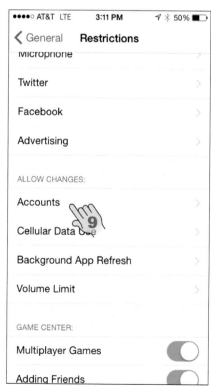

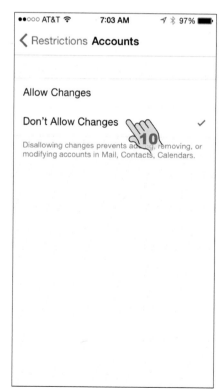

Instagram Privacy Settings & Reporting Abuse

Instagram is currently the most popular image/messaging social network among teens. It has straight forward privacy and abuse reporting features.

Setting Private Account

1. Open the Instagram App. Select the Profile icon.

2. Select Settings ⚙ icon.

3. Turn on (blue) **Private Account**.

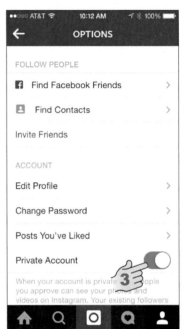

Reporting Abuse

4. Navigate to the account, image, or comment that you want to report as spam or abusive.

   Select ••• to open the Reporting sub-menu.

5. Follow the sub-menu prompts to the correct category

Twitter Privacy & Security Settings
Desktop

The settings below are for the strictest privacy settings. 1. Log into Twitter and click on your profile picture. 2. Select **Settings** from drop down menu. 3. Select **Security & Privacy**. 4. Choose **Send login verification requests to** [your mobile phone]

5. Check **Require Personal information to reset my password**.

6. Select **Do not allow anyone to tag me in photos**.

7. Check **Protect my Tweets**.

8. Uncheck **Add a location to my Tweets**.

9. Click **Delete all location information**

10. **Save Changes**

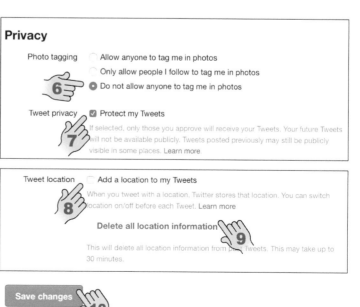

1. Open Twitter on your iOS device. Click on **Me**.

2. Select ☼ icon.

3. Select **Settings**.

4. Select your account.

5. Set all the privacy options as shown.

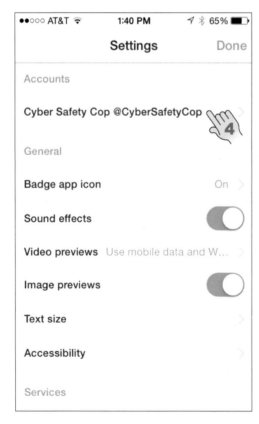

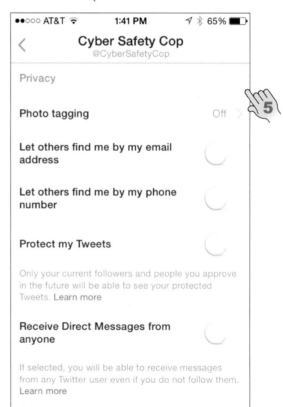

Facebook Privacy Settings

Do you think your child's Facebook page is private and secure? Can only approved friends see your child's personal information like the city they live in, birthday, or mobile phone number?

Use the steps below to test what your personal, or your child's, Facebook account looks like to a stranger.

1. Go to your profile and click ••• in the bottom right corner of the cover photo.
2. Click **View As**.

A truly private profile should display only the account name, profile image, and cover photo. If you see posts, pictures, or personal information you need to follow the directions on the proceeding pages.

Facebook Privacy Settings
Desktop Browser

1. Click the **downward arrow** in the right bottom corner of your cover photo.

2. Select **Settings**.

3. Select **Limit Past Posts** so your old post can only be seen by you and your friends.

   Select **Confirm**.

4. You can **Use Activity Log** to view all your posts, comments and likes. You can manage your old posts here, deleting them one-by-one. There is not a "delete all" option.

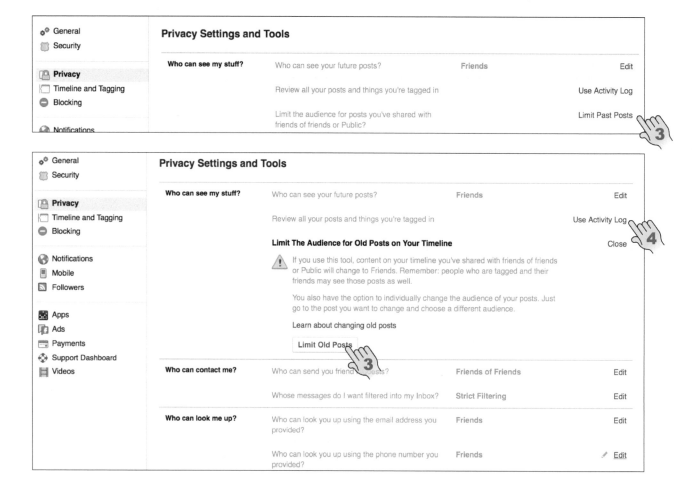

Facebook Privacy Settings

Desktop Browser Continued

> 5. In "Settings," select **Timeline and Tagging**. 6. Set to **Only Me** for strictest privacy setting. The settings below are the set to the most private options.

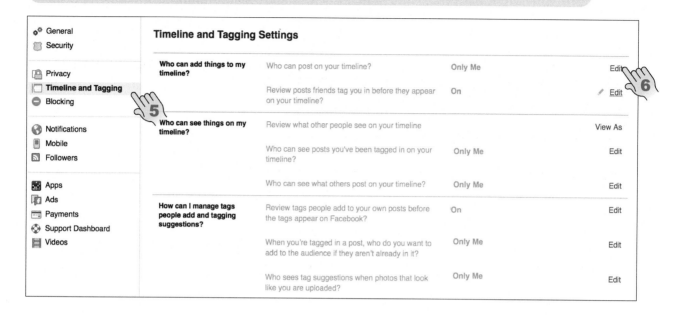

Facebook Privacy Settings iOS Mobile App

1. Click More ☰ in lower right menu.

2. Select **Account Settings**.

3. Select **Privacy**.

   Choose the same settings as the desktop browser version.

Android (not shown)

1. Click **More** symbol

2. Scroll down and select **Privacy Shortcuts**.

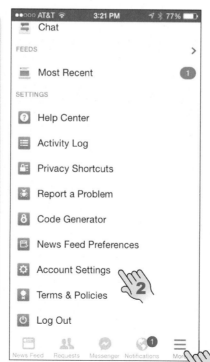

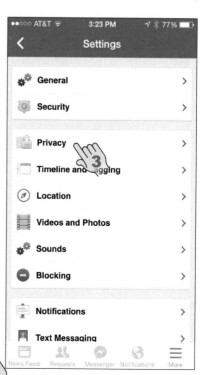

Facebook Blocking Abuse
Desktop Browser

1-2. Select **Settings** from drop down menu, 3. Select **Blocking**, 4. Type in the name or email of the person you want to block.

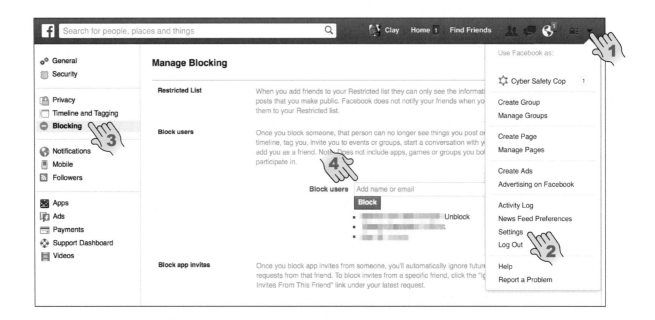

To block or report a comment,

5. Click on the **X** in the top right corner of the comment message box.

6. Select either **Report** or **Block**.

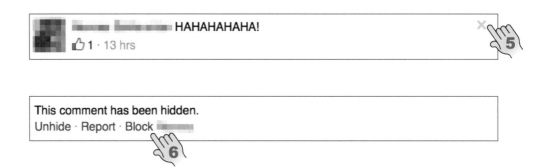

Facebook App Sharing Settings

Desktop Browser

1. Apps can share information and preferences. Their connections remain even after you delete the parent app off your device.

   From the settings menu, select **Apps**.

2. Delete apps that you are no longer using by clicking on the **X**.

3. Scroll down and select **Edit Apps Others Use**.

4. Uncheck information you don't want to share with other apps.

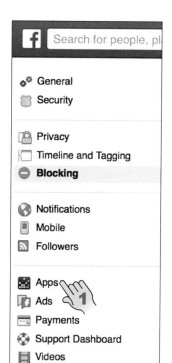

Eventbrite
✱ Custom

Apps Others Use

People who can see your info can bring it with them when they use apps. Use this setting to control the categories of information people can bring with them.

Edit

Apps Others Use   ✕

People on Facebook who can see your info can bring it with them when they use apps. This makes their experience better and more social. Use the settings below to control the categories of information that people can bring with them when they use apps, games and websites.

- Bio
- Birthday
- Family and relationships
- Interested in
- Religious and political views
- My website
- If I'm online
- My status updates
- My photos

- My videos
- My links
- My notes
- Hometown
- Current city
- Education and work
- Activities, interests, things I like
- My app activity

If you don't want apps and websites to access other categories of information (like your friend list, gender or info you've made public), you can turn off all Platform apps. But remember, you will not be able to use any games or apps yourself.

Cancel   Save

Facebook App Sharing Settings
iOS Mobile App

1. Click More ☰ in lower right menu.

2. Select **Account Settings**.

3. Select **Apps**.

4. Select **Logged in with Facebook**

5. Select the app you want to delete

6. Select **Remove App** at bottom on screen

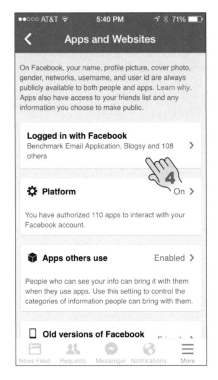

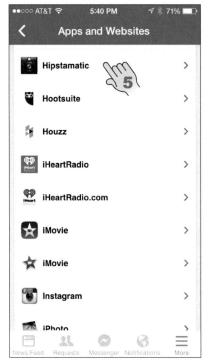

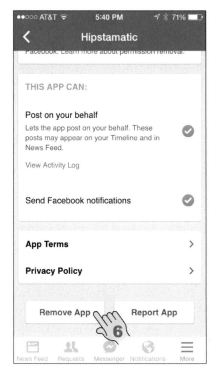

Facebook Messenger Privacy
Mobile Settings

Most of the privacy settings for Messenger can be managed through your Facebook profile on the browser or mobile platform.

1. Open Facebook Messenger mobile app and click the **Settings** cog icon.

2. Select **Privacy Policy**.

3. Select **Who can contact me**.

4. Select **Strict Filtering**

5. Scroll down to the bottom of the menu and select **More Settings**.

6. Select **Privacy**.

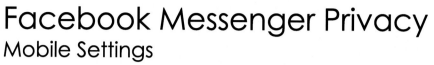

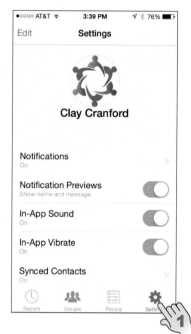

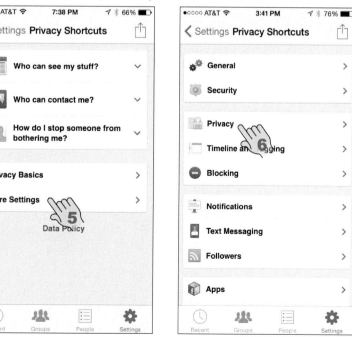

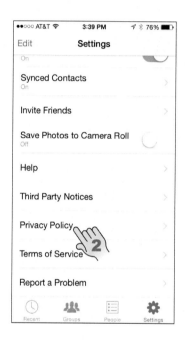

7. Select **Who can look you up using the email address you provided**.

8. Select **Friends**.

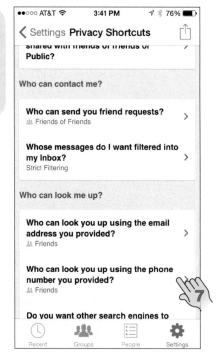

Syncing your device's contact with Facebook Messenger can open you up to being contacted by non-Facebook Friends. The instructions below will turn contact syncing off and delete all past synced contacts.

9. Open Settings menu and select **Synced Contacts**.

10. Select **Stop Syncing**.

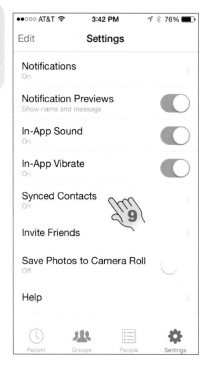

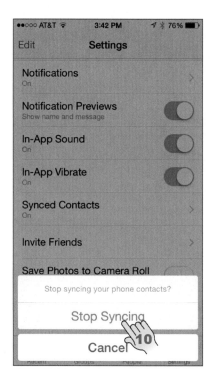

Facebook Messenger Blocking iOS

1. Select **Recent** messages.

2. Swipe across the contact right to left to reveal the sub-menu. To stop receiving messages from this contact, select **Mute**.

3. Select how long you want the contact muted.

4. To block report the sender as spam, select **More**.

5. Select **Mark as Spam**.

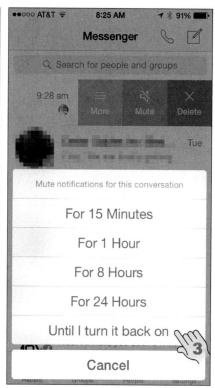

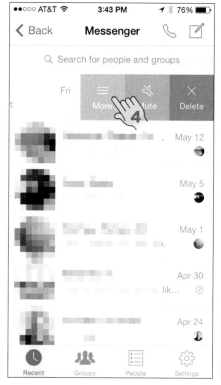

Facebook Messenger Blocking
Continued

6. To block the contact from both Facebook and Facebook Messenger, tap the profile picture from the message window.

7. Select **View Profile**.

8. Select ••• **More**.

9. Select **Block**.

Android OS (not shown)

1. Go to **Settings** and turn off **Synced Contacts**, and **Location**.

2. Select **Privacy** in the small print links at the bottom of the settings page.

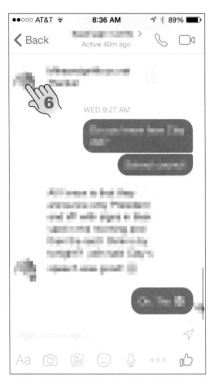

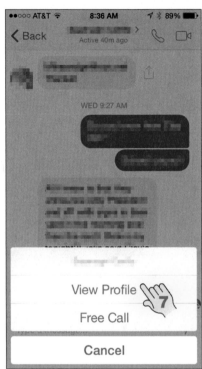

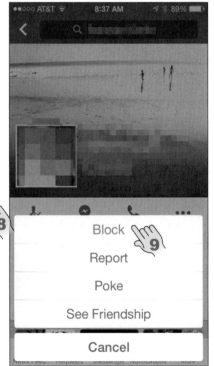

Skype Privacy & Security
Mac OS

These settings will make your Skype use more safe and secure by limiting your child's interaction with only the people on their contact list. Third party apps can record Skype video conversations. There is no way to stop another person from recording your conversation without your permission. Remind your child that even though they are talking to someone they know, they must behave in a way that would not embarrass them if everyone saw the conversation.

1. Open Skype, sign into your child's account. Do not link your child's Facebook account to Skype. Click **No thanks...**

2. Select **Preferences**.

3. Select **Privacy**.

4. Change all options to **Contacts** as shown.

5. Uncheck **Show my status on the web**.

Bring your Facebook friends into Skype

See their latest News Feed updates and call them in one click when you'd like to say hi. Learn more

Connect to Facebook

No thanks, I don't want to connect to Facebook right now

Skype	File	Edit	View	Con
About Skype				
Preferences... ⌘,				
Provide Skype Feedback...				
Check for Updates...				
Services ▶				
Manage API Clients...				
Hide Skype ⌘H				
Hide Others ⌥⌘H				
Show All				
Quit Skype ⌘Q				

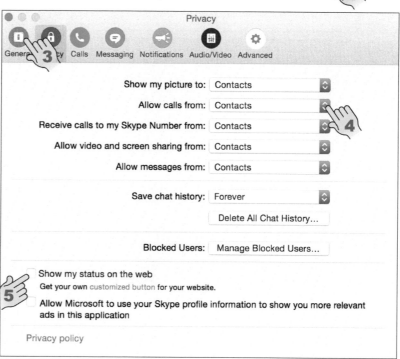

Privacy

General · Privacy · Calls · Messaging · Notifications · Audio/Video · Advanced

Show my picture to: Contacts

Allow calls from: Contacts

Receive calls to my Skype Number from: Contacts

Allow video and screen sharing from: Contacts

Allow messages from: Contacts

Save chat history: Forever

Delete All Chat History...

Blocked Users: Manage Blocked Users...

☐ Show my status on the web
Get your own customized button for your website.

☐ Allow Microsoft to use your Skype profile information to show you more relevant ads in this application

Privacy policy

Skype Privacy & Security

Mac OS Continued

6. To block a contact from contacting your child on Skype, click on **Contacts** on the left menu bar.

7. Right click anywhere on the contacts name to reveal the drop down menu.

8. Select **Block**.

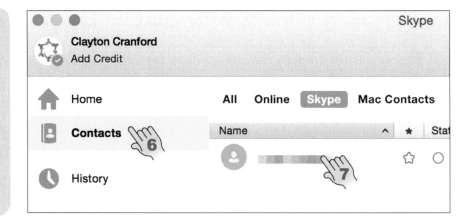

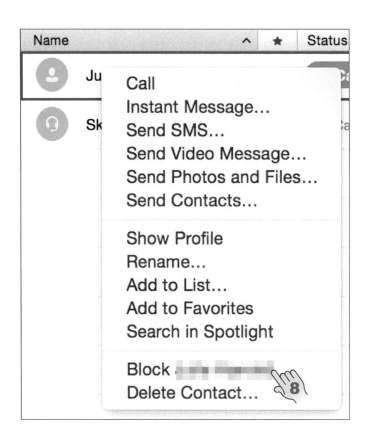

Skype Privacy & Security

Mac OS Continued

9. To prevent unintentionally downloading viruses or malware, turn off automatic downloads by Clicking on **General** in the Settings menu.

10. Uncheck **Automatically accept incoming files**.

11. Select **Advanced**.

12. Check **Allow direct connections to my contacts only**.

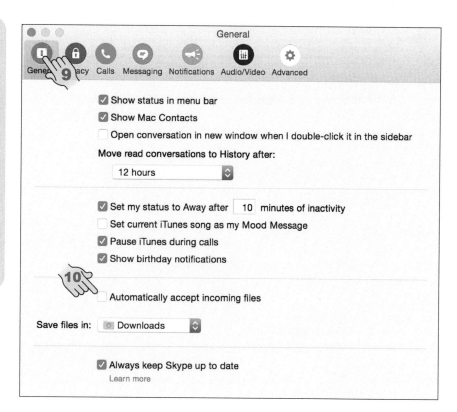

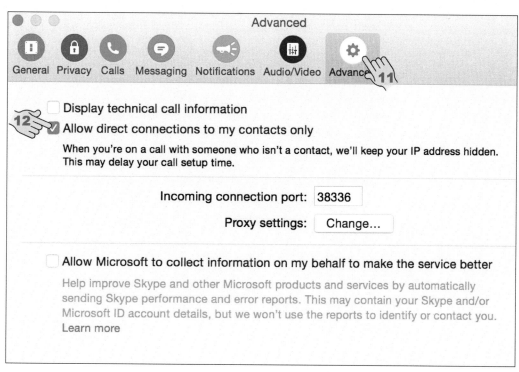

Skype Privacy & Security
iOS App

1. Tap on your profile picture.

2. Select **Settings**.

3. Turn off (white) **Automatically add friends**.

4. Select **Advanced**.

5. Turn on (green) **Allow direct connections to my contacts only**.

Android OS (not shown)

1. Tap on **Settings** in lower left menu bar.

2. Under **Contacts**, set **Automatically add friends** to **Don't use my address book**.

3. Under the **Privacy** menu, set **Allow IMs From** and **Receive Calls From** to **Contacts Only**.

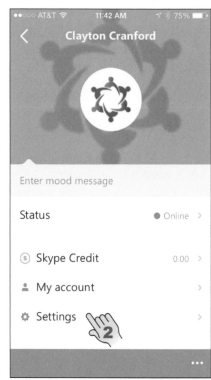

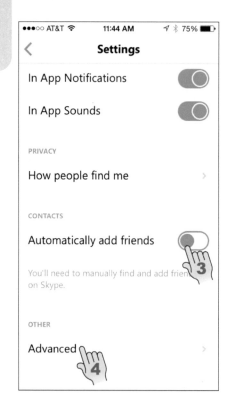

1. To block a contact on Skype, select **People** from the top navigation bar.

2. Tap on the contact that you want to block.

3. Tap on the contact's name in the top center position of the screen.

4. Tap on **...** to reveal the sub-menu.

5. Select **Bock**.

Android OS (not shown)

1. Tap on **People**.

2. Tap on the contact you wish to block.

3. Tap on their name in the top center portion of the screen.

4. Tap **Settings** in lower left menu.

5. Select **Block**.

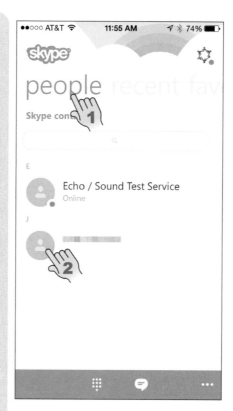

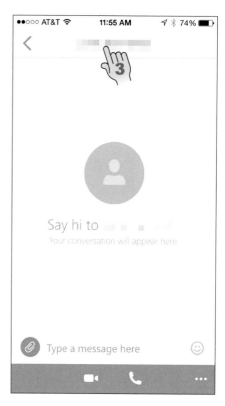

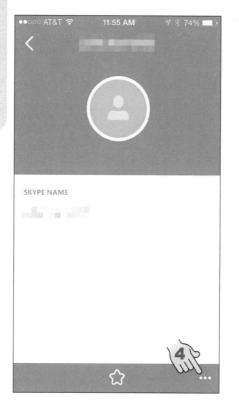

Social Media

1. Click on **Skype** in top menu bar.

2. Select **Privacy**.

3. Select **Privacy Settings**.

4. Click on Allow calls from **people in my Contact list only**.

5. Select **Save**.

To Block

1. Click on **Contacts**.

2. Right click on the name of the person you want to block.

3. Select **Block this Person**.

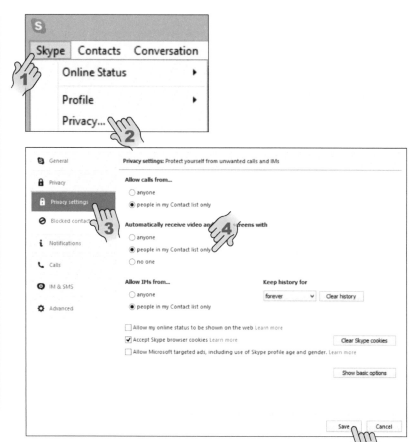

To Block

Reporting Bullying & Abuse

Social Media

Ask.fm
- URL of form to fill out: http://ask.fm/about/safety/safety-security-essentials

Badoo
- Report Abuse: https://badoo.com/feedback/
- Report User by clicking on his/her Profile and Selecting the "Report User" icon.

DeviantArt
- Report Abuse: http://help.deviantart.com/contact

Facebook
- The best way to report abusive content on Facebook is by using the Report link that appears near the content itself. Visit https://www.facebook.com/report for directions, complete with graphics, showing you how to report different types of abusive content (timelines, ads, events, groups, messages, pages, photos, videos, posts, etc).
- URL of form to fill out: https://www.facebook.com/help/contact/274459462613911
- Law enforcement: https://www.facebook.com/safety/groups/law/guidelines/

FourSquare
- Report Abuse: http://support.foursquare.com/anonymous_requests/new
- (Select "I want to Report a Violation" and Fill out Form)
- Law enforcement: http://support.foursquare.com/attachments/token/i3zateimclhxngy/?name=4sq+Law+Enforcement+Requests.pdf

Instagram
- How to Address Abuse: http://help.instagram.com/527320407282978
- Reporting abuse: http://help.instagram.com/165828726894770
- Abuse form to fill out: http://help.instagram.com/contact/570148369683854
- Blocking abusers: http://help.instagram.com/426700567389543
- Law enforcement: https://help.instagram.com/494561080557017

Keek
- Report Abuse email: feedback@keek.com
- Privacy, Spam, Malicious Violations email: privacy@keek.com
- To Report a User: Navigate to the "Bio" section of your account and Click on "Report User" at the bottom of the "Bio" section.

LinkedIn
- Report Abuse email: abuse@linkedin.com

MeetMe:
- Report Abuse: http://www.meetme.com/?mysession=bGlzdGluZ19ib2d1cw

MeetUp:
- Report Inappropriate Content and Spam: http://help.meetup.com/customer/portal/articles/1651883-how-to-report-inappropriate-content-and-spam
- Blocking Someone: http://help.meetup.com/customer/portal/articles/1651875-block-someone-from-contacting-me
- Report Abuse: http://help.meetup.com/customer/portal/emails/new or abuse@meetup.com

Pinterest
- URL of form to fill out: https://help.pinterest.com/anonymous_requests/new
- (Choose "Spam & Abuse" from the menu)
- URL with additional reporting information: https://help.pinterest.com/entries/22163668-Report-objectionable-or-spammy-content-comments-or-people#person
- Law enforcement: https://help.pinterest.com/entries/24009547-Pinterest-Law-Enforcement-Guidelines

Qooh.me
- Report Abuse: info@qooh.me

Reddit
- The report button, shown on all links and comments provides a way for you to report abusive content to the moderators.

Snapchat
- Report Inappropriate Content: https://support.snapchat.com/co/inappropriate
- Report Harassment: https://support.snapchat.com/co/harassment
- Report Hacked Account: https://support.snapchat.com/co/hacked-account
- Report Spam: https://support.snapchat.com/co/spam
- Report Other Abuse or Safety Issue: https://support.snapchat.com/co/other-abuse
- Law enforcement: http://info.publicintelligence.net/SnapchatLawEnforcementGuide.pdf

Spillit
- URL of form to fill out: http://www.spillit.me/support

Tagged
- Report A Profile: Select the "Report Profile" button next to the profile photo of the user and fill out the information required.
- Block a User: Select "Block User" link to the left of users profile photo

Tumblr
- phone: 678-439-8862
- URL for blocking abusers: http://www.tumblr.com/block
- email: abuse@tumblr.com
- Law enforcement: http://www.tumblr.com/docs/en/law_enforcement

Twitter
- URL to report an abusive user: https://support.twitter.com/forms/abusiveuser
- URL to report self harm:https://support.twitter.com/forms/general?subtopic=self_harm
- URL to report account impersonation:https://support.twitter.com/forms/impersonation
- Address: Twitter, Inc. 1355 Market Street, Suite 900 San Francisco, CA 94102
- Law enforcement: http://support.twitter.com/entries/41949-guidelines-for-law-enforcement#

Vimeo
- Report a Video: Click on Flag icon on the bottom right of the video in question.
- Report a Spam: http://vimeo.com/forums/help/topic:68617
- Report User: https://vimeo.com/help/contact

Vine
- To Report Abuse: https://vine.co/contact (Choose Abuse and fill out form)
- Vine Support Form: https://support.twitter.com/forms/vine
- To Report a Post: Click on the bottom right side button (…) and Click "Report Post"
- To Report a Spam or Block User: Click on user's name, then Click on the top right button (…), then click on "Report This Person" or "Report as Spam"

VK.com
- Report Abuse: support@vk.com

Whisper
- To Report Abuse: http://whisper.sh/legal

YikYak
- To Report Abuse: Click on the comment and Press "Report" on the upper right hand corner.
- Send an email with a screenshot of the comment attached to yikyakapp@gmail.com

YouTube
- URL of form to fill out to report abuse/cyberbullying: http://www.youtube.com/reportabuse
- Reporting content: http://support.google.com/youtube/bin/answer.py?hl=en&answer=2802027

Messaging Services

Kik
- Abuse information: https://kikinteractive.zendesk.com/entries/23518788-I-m-being-harassed-on-Kik-What-can-I-do-

- email: support@kik.com
- Mailing address: 420 Weber St North, Suite I, Waterloo, ON, N2L 4E7, CANADA
- Blocking abusers: https://kikinteractive.zendesk.com/entries/23510736-How-do-I-block-someone-
- Law enforcement: http://kik.com/lawenforcement/

ooVoo
- Report harassment: http://support.oovoo.com/link/portal/3908/4244/Article/1356/-How-do-I-report-harassment
- Block a contact on a Windows device: http://support.oovoo.com/link/portal/3908/4244/Article/1311/How-can-I-block-unblock-or-remove-contacts-on-my-PC
- Block a contact on a Mac device: http://support.oovoo.com/link/portal/3908/4244/Article/1310/How-can-I-block-unblock-or-remove-contacts-on-my-Mac

Skype
- Report/block a contact in Skype (Windows): https://support.skype.com/en/faq/FA10488/how-do-i-block-or-report-a-contact-in-skype-for-windows-desktop
- Report/block a contact in Skype (Apple): https://support.skype.com/en/faq/FA10870/how-do-i-manage-my-contacts-in-skype-for-mac-os-x#6
- URL of form to fill out: https://support.skype.com/en/faq/FA1170/how-can-i-contact-skype-customer-service?intcmp=SN-Mods

Text Plus
- Report abusive behavior: http://help.textplus.com/customer/portal/articles/140059
- Block a user: http://help.textplus.com/customer/portal/articles/660831-ios—how-to-block-users
- Flag inappropriate pictures and content for review: http://help.textplus.com/customer/portal/articles/551189
- Contact Safety, Security, and Privacy team: abuse@textplus.com

Viber
- Email: support@viber.com
- Report Abuse: http://helpme.viber.com/

WeChat
- Report Abuse email: support@wechat.com

WeHeartIt
- Report Abuse email: hello@weheartit.com
- Legal issues: legal@weheartit.com

WhatsApp
- Report Abuse email: support@whatsapp.com

Zello
- Report Abuse email: support@zello.com

Search Engines

Ask.com
- URL for help to deal with harassment: http://help.ask.com/ics/support/default.asp?deptID=30018&_referrer=http://www.ask.com/answers/browse?o=0&l=dir&qsrc=321

Bing
- URL of form to fill out: https://support.discoverbing.com/eform.aspx?productKey=bingsearchabuse&ct=eformts

Google
- URL of form to fill out: http://support.google.com/bin/static.py?hl=en&ts=1114905&page=ts.cs
- USA Toll Free phone: 1-877-355-5787
- Worldwide Toll Free phone: 1-404-978-9282
- Additional Phone: 650-253-0000

MSN (Hotmail, Skype, Passport, XBox, etc.)
- Report concern: http://technet.microsoft.com/en-us/security/cc165610.aspx
- Safety and Security Center for Families: http://www.microsoft.com/security/family-safety/default.aspx#Products
- Law enforcement: http://info.publicintelligence.net/MSN-Compliance.pdf

Yahoo
- URL of form to fill out: http://io.help.yahoo.com/contact/index?locale=en_US&y=PROD_ACCT&page=contact
- Customer Service phone: 866-562-7219 or 866-438-1582
- Law enforcement: https://www.eff.org/files/filenode/social_network/Yahoo_SN_LEG-DOJ.pdf

Cell Phone Service Providers

AT&T
- phone: 800-331-0500
- Email: abuse@att.net
- Email to report child exploitation: cp@abuse-att.net

Cricket Wireless
- phone: 1-800-Cricket (274-2538)
- URL to get help for harassment: http://www.mycricket.com/support

Sprint and BoostMobile
- phone: 888-211-4727
- Email to report security issues: security@sprint.net
- Email to forward abuse: abuse@sprint.net
- URL to report child exploitation: https://www.sprint.net/index.php?p=support_ce_request
- URL to report a security violation: https://www.sprint.net/index.php?p=support_report_scan

T-Mobile
- phone: 800-866-2453 or 877-453-1304

Verizon
- phone: 800-922-0204
- Email: abuse@verizon.com

Virgin Mobile
- phone: 1-888-322-1122
- URL of form to fill out: https://www1.virginmobileusa.com/about/prepareEmailUs.do

Internet Service Providers

AT&T
- phone: 800-331-0500
- Email: abuse@att.net
- Email to report child exploitation: cp@abuse-att.net

Brighthouse
- phone: 866-309-3279
- Email: abuse@rr.com
- Email to report spam: spamblock@security.rr.com

CenturyLink
- phone: 800-201-4099
- URL of form to fill out: https://www.centurylink.com/static/Pages/Support/ContactUs/escalationForm.html

Charter
- phone: 888-438-2427
- URL of general support: http://www.myaccount.charter.com/customers/support.aspx?SupportArticleID=51
- Report Cyberbullying: Copy and paste any evidence into an email and send to: abuse@charter.net

Comcast
- phone: 888-565-4329 (Customer Security Assurance Department)
- Report child pornography: CPReports@comcast.net
- Report cyberbullying: Copy and paste any evidence into an email and send to: abuse@comcast.net including the words "Harassment Investigation" in the subject line.
- email: abuse@comcast.net

Earthlink
- phone: 888-327-8454
- URL of general support: http://support.earthlink.net/articles/policy-procedures/how-to-report-fraud-junk-and-spam-emails.php
- email address to report fraud: fraud@abuse.earthlink.net

Qwest (Now part of CenturyLink)
- Email: abuse@qwest.com

Gaming

Club Penguin United
- URL of form to fill out: http://www.clubpenguinunited.com/home/report-something/

League of Legends
- Report Abuse: support@riotgames.com
- How and Why to Report: https://support.leagueoflegends.com/entries/21739510-Reporting-a-Player

Minecraft
- Report abuse: minecraft@minecraft.ign.com

NeoPets
- Report Abuse: http://www.neopets.com/autoform_abuse.phtml?abuse=account

Playstation Network
- phone: 800-345-SONY
- URL of form to fill out: http://np.us.playstation.com/

Pogo
- Report Abuse or Spam: http://help.ea.com/en/article/how-do-i-report-abuse-or-terms-of-service-violations-on-pogo/

Poptropica
- URL of form to fill out (for players): http://www.poptropica.com/contact/contact-players.html
- URL of form to fill out (for parents): http://www.poptropica.com/contact/contact-parents.html

Roblox
- Utilize the "Report Abuse" buttons located throughout the site. These Report Abuse buttons send a report directly to the moderators.
- Reporting abuse: Click "Menu" then click "Report Abuse", fill out form accordingly.
- Email: info@roblox.com

Webkinz
- To report something inappropriate in Kinz Chat, use the report tool (the tool like a shield).
- URL of form to fill out: http://support.ganzworld.com/webkinz-friends-cs-step-1/

Wii Network
- URL of form to fill out: http://www.nintendo.com/consumer/webform/

Words With Friends
- Report Abuse
  Email: admin@wordswithfriends.net (attach a screenshot of abuse)

World of Warcraft
- URL of form to fill out: https://us.battle.net/support/en/ticket/submit
- Law enforcement: http://info.publicintelligence.net/Blizzard2009.pdf

XBox Live
- URL of abuse reporting information: http://www.xbox.com/en-US/live/abuse/

Yahoo Games
- URL to get assistance: http://help.yahoo.com/kb/index?page=content&id=SLN6657&actp=search&viewlocale=en_US&searchid=1385424599462&locale=en_US&y=PROD_GAMES

Zynga
- Information on how to report abuse: http://company.zynga.com/security/frequently-asked-questions

Fraud and Scams

The Internet Crime Complaint Center (IC3)
The IC3 was established as a partnership between the Federal Bureau of Investigation (FBI) and the National White Collar Crime Center (NW3C) to receive Internet related criminal complaints and to further research, develop, and refer the criminal complaints to federal, state, local, or international law enforcement and/or regulatory agencies for any investigation they deem to be appropriate. http://www.ic3.gov/complaint/default.aspx

References

Giedd, J.N. et al. October 1999. "Brain development during childhood and adolescence: a longitudinal MRI study." Nature. Vol 2, No 10, pp. 861-863.

Brownlee, S. August 9, 1999. "Inside the Teen Brain." U.S.News.

Pew Research Center, "Teens, Social Media & Technology Overview 2015" April 9, 2015. http://www.pewinternet.org/2015/04/09/teens-social-media-technology-2015/

Harris Interactive, "Trends & Tudes 2007 Volume 6 Issue 4," April 2007. https://www.ncpc.mediaroom.com/.../Trends+%26+Tudes+-+Harris+Interactive.pdf

American Academy of Pediatrics, "Media and Children," https://www.aap.org/en-us/advocacy-and-policy/aap-health-initiatives/Pages/Media-and-Children.aspx

http://www.dailymail.co.uk/news/article-2888300/Is-child-s-new-iPad-magnet-paedophiles-Ten-year-old-girl-groomed-tablet-perverts-despite-parents-taking-sensible-safety-measures.html

National Crime Prevention Council, "Stop Bullying Before it Starts," http://www.ncpc.org/resources/files/pdf/bullying/cyberbullying.pdf

Department of Homeland Security, "Blue Campaign: Human Trafficking 101," http://www.dhs.gov/sites/default/files/publications/blue-campaign/bc-inf-ht101-blue-campaign-human-trafficking-101.pdf

Cyber Safety Cop Workshops

Cyber Safety Workshop for Parents

The Cyber Safety Cop Workshop for Parents is a two-hour seminar that will prepare parents to effectively supervise their child on social media sites and protect them from cyberbullying.

The class first explains the current technology and applications teens are using to access the Internet and social media networks. Secondly, current cyberbullying trends and real world examples that Clayton Cranford has investigated in schools are discussed. Lastly, participants will be given tools and an action plan that they can immediately begin using to help keep their children safe online.

- New and popular apps rated
- Current bullying trends
- Current impact of bullying in schools
- Risks associated with popular social media sites
- Sexting and online predators
- How to set expectations and consequences
- How to create balance with life & technology
- Online security considerations
- How to monitor online activity
- How to deal with a bully
- School discipline and legal issues

Participants will receive an Internet Safety Contract, Cyber Safety Guide, and Cyber Safety Checklist.

Cyber Safety for Law Enforcement and Educators

The Cyber Safety Cop Workshop for Law Enforcement and Educators is an eight-hour seminar that will provide an in depth look into how teens use social media apps and other social networking platforms. This course will also explore the unique threats that exist online: cyberbullying, impersonation, identity theft, sexting, sexual predators, human trafficking, digital reputation management, pornography, and other high-risk behaviors. Effective tools and resources to properly supervise children online will be discussed. The attendee will also learn methods and strategies they can use to guide parents and students towards safer online practices.

Course Topics:

- Live demonstrations of the most popular social media applications
- Current impact of bullying in schools
- Risks associated with popular social media sites
- Sexting and online predators
- How to set expectations and consequences
- Online security considerations
- How to monitor online activity
- School discipline and legal issues

Each attendee will receive the Cyber Safety Cop Parent's Guide to Cyber Safety, Cyber Safety Checklist, Internet Safety Contract, as well as online tools and resources. This course is imperative for law enforcement, educators, and school psychologists to understand the profound affect social media has on a teen's life and how it impacts their safety.

Cyber Safety Cop Workshops

Cyber Safety Workshop for Students

Cyber Safety Cop Workshop for Students is a 45 minute interactive presentation aimed at students 5th to 12th grade.

It can be taught in a small classroom or in a gymnasium to hundreds of students at a time. Cyber Safety for Students gives each student the information they need to make good decisions in their digital lives. Additionally, the Cyber Safety class will show them common vulnerabilities to their safety and how they can make their social networks more secure. The program focuses on the importance of a positive digital reputation, and the long term impact of cyberbullying and sexting can have on their lives.

Cyber Safety for Students complements Cyber Safety for Parents. The concepts covered in the Student class are explained in the parent class, allowing parents to follow up with their children and reinforce what they learned at school.

How to Find or Host a Cyber Safety Cop Workshop Near You

Visit the Cyber Safety Cop website and check the events calendar to see if a workshop will be held in your city. www.cybersafetycop.com/events

Contact Clayton Cranford at info@cybersafetycop.com to inquire about having him bring the Cyber Safety Workshop to your school or community group.

Cyber Safety Cop Newsletter

Cyber Safety Cop's free newsletter provides parents with timely and critical information:

- Parent tips
- Tutorials on securing computers and mobile devices
- Reviews on new social media apps
- Online training
- How to deal with bullying
- Monthly newsletter
- How to use parental controls
- Upcoming workshops near you

Sign up for Cyber Safety Cop's free newsletter at www.cybersafetycop.com

About the Author

CLAYTON CRANFORD IS
The Cyber Safety Cop

Clayton Cranford is a law enforcement professional based in Southern California. Clayton is one of the nation's leading law enforcement educators on social media and child safety. He created Cyber Safety Cop, an Internet and social media safety program. It teaches parents and students how to avoid the inherent risks of social media and other web based platforms by using safe habits.

Clayton has more than 20 years of teaching experience and has been a featured speaker at the National Conference on Bullying, the Southwest Conference on Human Trafficking, the California Association of Crime Prevention Officers, and the National Association of School Resource Officers.

Clayton was awarded the 2015 National Bullying Prevention Award from the School Safety Advocacy Council, and the 2015 American Legion Medal of Merit for his bullying prevention work.

Clayton is a sought-after media commentator on cyber safety and child safety issues. He has appeared on several TV shows, "The Doctors," NBC News, and CBS News.

Clayton has partnered with Agape International Missions (AIM), a leader in the fight against child sex trafficking in Cambodia. Clayton has served overseas with AIM in Cambodia's child sex trafficking epicenter and speaks at various Human Trafficking symposiums and conferences, spreading awareness and providing families with important safety information.

Clayton is married with two boys who love the Internet and technology. Clayton has a Bachelor's Degree in Philosophy and a Master's Degree in Criminal Justice.

Made in the USA
San Bernardino, CA
14 May 2017